TRUE UNITY

TRUE UNITY

WILLING COMMUNICATION
BETWEEN HORSE AND HUMAN

by
TOM DORRANCE

Edited by Milly Hunt Porter

Library of Congress No. 87-072039
ISBN 1-884995-09-8

First printing November 1987

Twelfth printing March, 1998

ISBN 1-884995-09-8

Published by
Give-It-A-Go Enterprises
P.O. Box 248 • Bruneau, ID 83604

In association with

8386 N. Madsen Avenue
Clovis, California 93611
(209) 322-5917

Manufactured in the United States

Table of Contents

Introduction

By Bill Dorrance

One thing about Tom, he never liked to be in trouble himself or have trouble with the horses or stock that he was handling. That's probably why he spent as much time as he did trying to figure out horses.

There were eight children in the family, four boys and four girls. The ranch where we grew up was in Wallowa County, the northeastern corner of Oregon, about fifty miles from the Idaho line and about the same from the Washington line. Dad went in there in 1882, and homesteaded on Crow Creek when he was a young fellow. Mother taught school there.

When Margaret and Lillian grew up and finished school, they taught school, too. Jean and Ethel did secretarial work.

Our dad spent his time with the business of cattle and farming, about two hundred and fifty purebred cows and about five hundred head of commercial Hereford cattle. None of the animals Dad worked with ever seemed to have a lot of problems. They all respected him, but there wasn't fear.

We boys were just kind of turned loose with the saddle horses. We didn't have many when we were small. It wasn't like we had a whole bunch, but we had a few. The saddle horse breaking was pretty much left to the boys. Jim was the oldest. He was six years older than I. My brother Fred was a couple of years younger than I. Tom was next to Fred, three years younger. Sometimes Fred and I would get into a disagreement and we weren't above trying to get the other fellow down. When it looked too serious to Tom, he would try to do all he could to get us to stop. He never liked to see trouble, regardless of where it was.

The first colt I remember Jim rode, Dad led for him; I don't know how old Jim was; I suppose he was about twelve. As Jim grew older, he never seemed to have fear of any horse, regardless of how rough the country was, and the horses never seemed to be worried about him. He looked real nice on a horse, even a bucking horse; not many got out from under him. When I started to ride the colts, if I couldn't ride one I always felt Jim could. He was quite a help to me. I remember the first colt I had was kind of a gentle one. It just jumped out a little bit. I wondered how anyone stayed on a bucking horse.

We all liked to work with the livestock. I don't remember anyone saying much about how you handle a horse. We just got the horse in the corral and roped him and got him halter broken. We got the saddle on him some way or other. We were just kids. The colts were fairly young. They probably were three years old or older. I don't know as we rode any younger than that, because of the miles the horses needed to cover. Most horses were not started very young. If someone had a horse he wanted ridden, we got five to ten dollars for riding the horse for three

Haying in Oregon about 1920

viii

or four months. That was quite a lot of money in the early 1920s.

Putting up hay was a big part of the summer work in those days. It was all done with teams of horses. There were no tractors or trucks on the place until 1943. The hay was brought in from the field on slips. A derrick was used to stack hay. Driving derrick team was usually a job for a younger kid. For several summers that was Tom's job.

In the summer some of the cattle were driven to the forest, while others were kept in various pastures. Some of these pastures were close to home, others five miles up the creek, or about five miles on down the creek.

The purebred cattle needed close attention. Usually whoever was doing that would go in one direction in the forenoon and the other direction from home in the afternoon. When Tom was real young he often went with one of us other boys. When Jean got to where she could drive derrick team, looking after cattle on some of the pastures got to be Tom's job. He started to learn and memorize each cow and her tattoo number; in a few years he knew them all by heart.

After we had gotten some of the colts we were riding going pretty nice, often Tom would ride one of those out, checking the pasture.

Sometimes folks would come by and ask how their horse was doing. "Well," we'd say, "Tom's riding him." It looked pretty good for the horse if a little ole kid could ride him.

We usually halter broke our own colts in the spring as yearlings before we turned them on the forest range. If we got colts from someone else, sometimes they weren't halter broken. Some of them were older and really wild.

In 1924, Dad got a government remount thoroughbred stallion for three years, and kept a stud colt of his out of a thoroughbred mare. He also had a draft stallion at that time. Soon the horse numbers built up to about one hundred and fifty head.

In 1926 Fred wanted to work out, so he went over to Snake River and worked for two years on a cattle outfit. Jim bought a place of his own on Snake River in 1927. In 1928 Fred went to Nevada and worked on some of those large ranches. He worked with some good hands while he was there. Some were older men that hadn't done much but ride. Fred was soon riding rough string and got a lot of good experience while he was there. Fred was a fellow that didn't do a lot of talking, but if he watched someone doing something better than he, he

William Church Dorrance, 1937

Minnie Tinsley Dorrance, 1937

Mom with the girls, c. 1935

Dad with the boys, c. 1935

William C. Dorrance, Tom's father, still riding at ninety

Barn and house built at Crow Creek in 1915

could see what was taking place. It didn't make much difference what it was. He was interested in a lot of things, but liked to work with cattle and horses best. Once when Dad was sick, Fred came home for a week or so, and told us about some of those things.

Fred stayed in Nevada a couple of years, then went to California. A year or two later I went to California. By then Tom was the only one of us boys still at home. He worked alone a lot with the cattle and horses and got to know their ways. The horses from the thoroughbred stallion were mostly pretty good. With so many of those horses on the ranch Tom didn't take in outside horses.

Tom was easy with the horses, and they all worked for him. He wanted to get along with them. As time went on Tom figured out how to get a relaxed feel with horses. Not many of his horses bucked, but if one should it wasn't liable to get out from under him. That relaxed feel really felt good to Tom and the horse.

In 1945 the folks sold the original homestead at Crow Creek. They kept the place at Joseph, which they had bought in 1917. The folks passed away in the 1950s and the rest of the Oregon property was sold in 1960.

The next few years Tom was able to travel some and spent time helping different people with problems with their horses.

I went over with Tom the first day he went to help Ray Hunt with his horse, Hondo. Ray had met Tom at the fair in Elko, Nevada, the fall before, and had told him about the horse. Tom wasn't in California long that year. That was twenty-six years ago.

Tom was always wondering if there wasn't a better way of helping the person understand the horse. The people he was helping seemed to be getting quite a lot out of it. Many times he said it seemed like he was getting more from it than the person he was trying to help.

In 1966 Tom married Margaret and he has lived in California since that time.

For several years Tom had had an idea for an automatic gate. When he retired from being involved in ranching full time, he had more time to devote to developing the gate.

Before Tom was ready to market the gate, he installed an experimental gate at my place. It's been there ten years now and is still working real good. Just the other day I noticed on the counter it has opened 28,000 times.

Tom is still helping different folks with their horses. In May 1985, Merced College gave him a plaque in appreciation for the help he had given their horse classes.

Prologue

By Milly Hunt Porter

From the beginning of time, history has been sprinkled with individuals who, because of something unique in their personalities, take the very ordinary in their environments and see in it, or do with it, a little more than others seem to have gotten from the same opportunities.

Sometimes years of formal study precede each step forward, until finally, when the thoughts and feelings are collected into book form to be shared by others, many sources can be quoted as reference material.

A quarter of a century ago, because of a horse with special problems, I became acquainted with a person with special talents for understanding and helping horses. Born and raised on a ranch, during a half century of living with livestock he had learned to recognize and appreciate the uniqueness in each animal. It was evident that he was able to approach each animal, especially those with man-made problems, with a gift of acceptance and the assurance of the true worth of the animal. The troubled horse, *especially*, would come to respond with the same sort of respect. All who watched these exchanges could recognize the evident communication and understanding between the man and the horse.

As fence rail observers and riders watched these exchanges, their problem became one of understanding what they were observing. It seemed that it was easier for this man to communicate with the horses than it was for him to communicate his thoughts and feelings about the horses with the other riders. It was not a question of not wanting to share with others what he saw and felt in a horse, for he always tried to help both the horse and the rider. It was a question of finding the words.

In working with a horse and rider, he would organize the situation in such a way (by voice instruction and body movement) that his desired result would occur. At just that instant he would exclaim, "Do you feel that?" The rider may have realized a change, but still may not really have recognized even a fraction of what had actually happened.

There have been many steps forward for the riders who began to learn from Tom Dorrance so long ago. As their ability to recognize and meet their horses' needs have grown, so has their awareness of how much there is to learn. They keep coming back to Tom for advice and encouragement. For many of these riders the first thing they remember Tom saying, after "Do you feel that?" was, "It's feel, timing, and balance we're working for." Tom still says he can't improve much on that explanation, but through the years this man, who seems to talk to horses, has begun to verbalize a lot more for his riders. It has not been easy, because of the complexities involved in attempting to express the quicksilver qualities of the intricate communication between horse and rider. It is even more difficult to capture these experiences in book form.

The first riders Tom helped would sometimes ask Tom if there was anything in print he could suggest they read. His answer then was, "There may be, but I have not read it yet*." When he was pressed for the source of his understanding, I've heard him say, "I guess I learned it from the horse!"

This book is an attempt to share a bit of what Tom has learned from the horse.

---

*Years later Tom read *Kinship With All Life* by J. Allen Boone and *Dressage* by Henry Wynmalen, M.F.H.; he since often suggests riders read both books.

Getting It Together

People often ask how I have gotten it together for myself and the horse. I'll make an attempt to answer. I was born on May 11, 1910, near Joseph, Oregon. As I look backward through the years of my life there have been hundreds of people and horses that have helped me develop my understanding of the *True Unity and Willing Communication Between Horse and Human.*

Our father and mother were good people with good standards that they tried to pass on to their children. The family was always good to me. I always felt freedom. By that I don't mean that I could do as I pleased about everything or anything. There were guidelines, standards and responsibilities for me to operate within. I had the freedom to explore and experiment so I could develop my own character. I believe that could have been the foundation for me to find, as I worked with animals, that this was as important to the animals as it had been to me.

The sixth born of the eight children, I had the benefit of the older brothers and sisters' experiences, and they were pretty handy kids. As I grew a little older it seemed interesting to watch the neighbors and how they handled different little things. Jess Foster was one I liked to watch work in the blacksmith shop. He worked fast—things just seemed to shape up. The winter I was three and a half years old Jess and my Dad built a bob sled—I liked to watch. Jess was good at shoeing horses and building fence; he was an all-around handyman.

Dan Warnock was another neighbor who was an interesting person for me. The Warnocks were a large family also (nine children). Dan raised cattle and lots of horses. Dan could get a horse going with very little handling. He raised them to sell, and he sold—he was a good

Tom and his dog at Crow Creek in 1917

businessman. His youngest son, Danny, rode his father's race horses when he was real young—Danny was a good little rider and a real good kid.

Cliff Wade was another good neighbor and a real good friend. He was a person I enjoyed working with and being around. He was twenty-one years older than I—so I had the benefit of those twenty-one years of his experience. Cliff was good with horses and mules. He had a lot of understanding of a horse. When I was young I liked to listen to Cliff visit with other people about horses; he always had an open mind. In the late 1940s Cliff sold his ranch operation in Wallowa County and was out of the county most of the time for several years. Then when Cliff was seventy-two years old he and I got together for a couple of weeks and started several young horses. Cliff hadn't lost any of the savvy of his younger days—but I had made some progress on some of the finer points we had both by-passed earlier. Cliff was quick to pick up on them and put them to use, once he saw how important they were to the horse and person.

It would be very difficult for me to talk about working with people and their horses without Ray Hunt becoming involved.

Ray Hunt and his horse

It will soon be twenty-seven years since I first met Ray Hunt—that has been another fortunate experience of my life. I have never experienced anyone who could pick up on the slightest clue and build on it in the right direction in such a short time—it is as if he has been doing it all his life.

Ray was doing well before I met him. All I did, maybe, for Ray was help him realize how much potential he really had and how he could put it to work for himself in so many ways. I soon realized this was an opportunity I was searching for. Soon I was asking Ray the *almost* impossible and he would do it. This got real exciting for Ray, and I was having the time of my life. Ray never seems to tire of my nonsense. As good as Ray was before we met—it seemed he was bursting at the seams for a way he could get these itchy spots to going for him—all I had to do was point out where to scratch. Ray has been scratching ever since.

I sold the last of my property in Wallowa County, Oregon, April 1960, bought a small house trailer and set out to see and do some of the things I had dreamed about. Soon I was at the 25 Ranch near Battle Mountain, Nevada. My oldest brother, Jim, was there. The 25 Ranch was owned and operated by the Marvel family. The ranch had lots of horses, cattle and sheep. Dick, the oldest Marvel brother, was superintendent of the sheep operation. Tom and John were with the cattle and horse operation. It was interesting to have an opportunity to get better acquainted and really get to know this family, the father, mother, three sons and their families. I will always have fond memories of the days I spent there.

I sort of divided my time between the 25 Ranch, Wallowa County, Oregon, and California, along with other trips and places for about five years. Then a lady who pretended to have a horse problem entered my life. In 1966 she got me blindfolded, haltered, hogtied and saddled. By the time I discovered what had happened, it was too late. But you know that was the best thing that ever happened to me.

The foregoing events have all been important in helping me understand horses and what makes them tick. But the part that has meant the most to the horse and me is the communication between us. This is the part where I really had to devote a lot of thought. I have watched horses when they are loose by themselves or loose in a group; gentle raised or wild range raised, their naturalness will show. And by

Tom and Margaret in June 1987

Marriage

In a hoss they call it loco,
In a man they call it love—
Spillin' milk while readin' mash notes
Written by a turtle dove.
He talks about her night and morning,
Raves about her to the cow
Till the critter kicks the bucket.
Well, you just can't blame her, can you now?
He used to be a top hand cowpoke,
Straight and girl-shy to a fault,
Till ole cupid got him hog tied,
And now he just ain't worth his salt.
What loco does to hosses
Is what love's sweet pison does to men,
And it takes a shock like sudden marriage
Till they find their wits again!
                                        —Unknown

studying their actions and reactions I have been helped to understand how to present myself in such a way that the horses will respond to what I may ask of them. This I believe is true nature.

This is something I have had to develop in myself, for myself, by myself. The True Unity and Willing Communication between the horse and me is not something that can be handed to someone—it has to be *learned*. It has to come from the inside of a person and the inside of a horse.

I believe horses *naturally* have tremendous faith in the human being. It is their natural instinct of self-preservation that the person needs to understand in order to gain the confidence of the horse. Many, many times I have seen where the person has missed the understanding of the horse's need for self-preservation and this has caused the lack of confidence the horse is trying so hard to gain. Then, if a person can present himself or herself to the horse in a way that is understandable to the horse, so it can develop confidence, I find the horse is so forgiving.

I wish I could describe the picture to you of what I see in a horse as I look at him and watch him and try to see him as he is, *A Horse*. I try not to think of him as anything other than a horse. In watching horses I try to let them tell me what is going on within themselves. There are so many things to try to bring out, it's hard to get it separated and get it in order, so that people understand. When I say I want the person to think of the horse as *A Horse*, some people might think that isn't much, but I am trying to bring out that that horse is *really, really* something special in his own uniqueness. I'm trying to stress the importance *of the horse*, of really seeing that horse as a horse, of seeing what he is and his potential.

I don't expect many horses will be reading this book to dispute or verify my feelings. I don't know how many folks will. I would like to think I could present my thoughts to folks in such a way that I could share with them my feelings about the horse, that I could get them to see and feel what I feel and see, that it would be a shared experience, *a willing communication.*

Most of the folks I meet who ask me for a little help with their horses are good, "trying" kinds of people. They are striving to understand their horses and the problems they are aware of. I try to work with them just where they are, at their awareness level. Then we build from there. I want to help the person to be able to approach his or her horse with acceptance, assurance and understanding; to work towards *true unity*. And I try to offer the person the same.

Through the years I have worked with so many riders who have given me their best, their time, their attention and their willing effort. We've worked together through these shared experiences that have been so valuable in my search for ways to build greater unity for the horse and the rider. I'm not going to try to name each person, but you know who you are; you know I am thinking of you and your horse and what we worked on together, and I sure do thank you for the privilege.

Down Memory's Lane With You

I'd like to ride down Memory's Lane
　　Together, you and I—
And sing the songs we used to sing
　　In the pleasant days gone by.
Our thoughts will bloom like flowers
　　And we'll gather every one;
We'll laugh at things we used to do,
　　The joyous things we've done.
And then someday if God is good
　　Perhaps beneath the sky—
Hand in hand we'll ride once more
　　Together—YOU AND I!

　　　　　　　　—Unknown

"Feel the Whole Horse"

The older I get the more it's beginning to dawn on me how most people seem to have so little *feel of the whole horse*—of what's going on in what part. Maybe, overall, they have a pretty good idea, but they don't know about this little spot here and that little spot there. Any one of them can be a good little spot, or it can be a bad little spot. People may have an idea what comes out of it, but what's really going on through all of this they don't recognize. Let me tell you what I think is essential to understand.

When I observe people and horses, it often seems to me that when the horse is trying to avoid something, or maybe is not doing what the rider asks of him, it is because the horse's sense of self-preservation is immediately taking effect. This may seem as though the horse does not want to cooperate. But the rider needs to recognize the whole horse: the horse has a basic need for self-preservation.

Often when working with riders and their horses, I will mention the need for self-preservation; this to me includes the physical and the mental—and a third factor. I've been trying for some time to think of words to get this third factor to where it comes to light; to show how it blends in with the other two—the physical and the mental. It is the least mentioned, but I am beginning to believe it is the most important factor to recognize: the rider needs to recognize the horse's need for self-preservation in Mind, Body, and, the third factor, *Spirit*. He needs to realize what that means to the horse so he can benefit from what it is in the horse, what it means to the horse. He needs to realize *how the person's approach can assure the horse that he can have his self-preservation and still respond to what the person is asking him to do.*

That is going to be a useful thing to both the person and the horse.

As I think back through the years, I don't know if I have really gotten this thing that I'm talking about clear for anyone that I have worked with. Some people have put some part of it to use, and they use that much to drift over the part they don't have. I'll add right on to that—I don't know how much there is I haven't discovered yet—how much there is *that could be.*

It seems to go in pieces. That's how it seems to go even for a horse. There's a "time" in there; it's just as well not to crowd the horse if he isn't ready for it. You keep offering, trying to help as much as you can, without troubling him too much about it. Then, there will be a day when it will just clear right up. I think it's a lot the same with the person.

This morning while we were feeding, I was observing this baby colt. It's a little over a week old now. It was lively when it came. The second day it played quite a bit; then the third and fourth day it found out it could do all kinds of running around. Then it got real curious; it would see us when we came in to feed. Its curiosity was really working. It was alert, and it was wanting to explore; but that self-preservation was strong. It was pretty careful, but its curiosity was just bubbling over.

When Margaret and I were feeding the mares, the colt was pretty uneasy, and the mother was protective. When it was right young, she wouldn't have wanted us bothering it at all. This time she was putting up with us because she knew we were not trying to hurt the colt. The colt was still wanting to make that contact, but self-preservation wouldn't quite allow it. He would get to about a certain point—stand there by his mother, kind of uneasy—then he had to go somewhere, you see. Then he would get out away from his mother a little farther, because we were beside her. We didn't try to do anything; the colt would come back. Then after a few trips like that, short trips, he took a longer trip. He just acted like he'd left home. He went out around, but he didn't stay put at any one place very long. We just waited there, and he came back. Well, each time, and especially those bigger trips, the colt felt more secure when he got back. He didn't feel secure when he was out there by himself. Finally, we did get to touch him and scratch him a little, but he was still uneasy.

The next morning there was a *big* change. The third morning the colt was looking forward to us. He was a little skeptical, but he could start away and make a recovery and find his way back. I think today is the fifth day of this, and he's looking forward to us. He will come out to meet us. Then we can pet him and scratch him, and he will follow us. And all this time the mother knows where he is, and as long as it's us, she can keep eating.

A mare seems to like for her colt to get attention. I've noticed that in the past; they are very protective of the colt when it is right young. But, as the colts get a little older, if they can do a little exploring and get a little attention, I think mares are like any other mother: they are proud of their young, and they like for them to get some attention.

This morning the colt followed me out about seventy-five feet from the feeder. He was getting pretty brave to be on his own so much.

Many people don't realize how easy it is to destroy this confidence the horse has built up in the human—the closeness between the horse and person. If the person will allow the horse to use this confidence and closeness, it will be strong in the horse. But the person generally doesn't realize what the horse is trying to apply—what it's really wanting the person to grasp. That is very seldom recognized by the person, but the horse is chuck full of it.

Generally people have no idea what I'm talking about, so we need to try to figure out some way to understand this thing the horse is so full of, and that he has such a strong desire to get from the person in return. We are searching for, and trying to find, some way to get this into print, so people will be able to put it to use for the benefit of themselves and their horses. It has to be a *togetherness*.

I used to mention "approach" and "unity" in trying to explain this concept. But, as I look on it now, people heard the words but were not getting much out of it or getting the picture clear enough. You might say, they would put their ears up a little (I'm speaking of the people) when I would mention it, as if it might have been new terminology for them. But if I would try to elaborate on it, they generally would just wait until I got on to something else, without trying to let it penetrate.

If we can find a way to bring this to the surface, people would realize what to start working for. Then it would turn on a light for them; it would hold their attention. They could start to realize what the horse is really trying to do. Without that understanding we might just as well throw the whole thing in the creek.

People try to crowd too much on themselves for the time they have. I keep telling them, not necessarily to try to get it to work for them *today*, but to try to figure out what is taking place. They need to feel there is something there that they have never recognized before. Or, there may be things that have been mentioned, some things that have taken place and that the persons noticed, but didn't know how to interpret at the time. Still it may have stuck in their minds; they just didn't know how to benefit from it. The important thing is that it doesn't matter if it comes out real good or real bad. The important thing is to try to understand what took place that caused it to be good or not so good. There's something about that: if a person can understand what took place, then maybe he can help the horse get in a position that will come out better, that will help him avoid getting into a position that's not so good. There's such a variation of situations that you can't say, "Do this and you get that."

People have to rely on themselves. I tell people that it has to come right out of the inside of themselves, the end result.

There can be some direction, or support and encouragement, but the *feel* itself can come from no one but themselves; they will know when the feel actually becomes effective, and when they are understanding.

I've looked in dictionaries for the definition for the word *feel*. I haven't been really satisfied with the definitions I've found for this thing I'm talking about with the horse—this thing *between the horse and the person*. When I talk to people about this *feel* and the *timing*, I realize how difficult it may be for them to try to get what I'm trying to say.

Some people will ride a horse as long as the horse lives and they will never get what I try to get just as early as I can, for a foundation. I don't mean that I'm trying to get everything completed, but to get enough there to where if the horse gets troubled he will come to me; or to where I can get him to come to me for security and cover. Without that foundation I feel very insecure with a horse. I've seen people just ride on by that foundation, and most of them survive. If they get a horse and don't build this foundation, then nothing will work at all. Then, in order for them to survive, they get rid of the horse. That is the smart thing for them to do; they shouldn't bother. But that horse might be real good material if he had a chance to develop in the way I've described.

I've found, for myself anyway, that I need to think of just where the horse is: what things bother him?

Sometimes the horse doesn't seem to understand, but it doesn't seem to bother him too much. Other horses, if they don't understand—they get bothered all over. So, there again, it's the individual variation.

The best thing I try to do for myself is to try to listen to the horse. I don't mean let him take over. I listen to how he's operating: what he's understanding or what he doesn't understand; what's bothering him and what isn't bothering him. I try to *feel* what the horse is *feeling* and operate from where the horse is.

This is what I'm trying to get riders to do, to operate from where the horse is instead of trying to operate from where the *rider* is. Usually, the horse is supposed to do everything the rider decides to do. *I like to work from where the horse is, to get him to be able to operate wherever and whenever I need him.*

The longer I live, the more I see in animals—about how they operate. No horse wants to be hurt. They will do things that will cause themselves to get hurt, but they usually don't head for that—that isn't what their intention is. They are no different from the rest of us. They have a strong sense of self-preservation.

Self-preservation comes in there real strong with horses and everything that lives. It's strong that way or there wouldn't be any horses. They would have faded out years ago.

For example, you can see two horses get into a fight, and neither one of them likes to get hurt, but they are still exposing themselves to the possibility of hurt and injury. When they get in a fight, each one of them figures on the other one yielding. The opposite horse is really coming into his own pressure. He will give this other horse some warning, and if that horse will yield, there is no fight.

In working with a horse, a lot of people get along pretty well until they go to training that horse. They need to understand how to set this training up, to be like horses naturally are when they get in a fight.

That gets kind of deep for people, but it's very effective. For a while people may not have it thought out and separated, and they may want to hurt the horse instead of letting him come into his own pressure. Sometimes people think punishment is the way to discipline the horse. The horse can only watch and resent that. But if it is presented as if he did it to himself, he will respect that. Then he will respond from your directing without any ill feeling.

Now, the horse doesn't really want to hurt anybody, but, if the directing isn't understood, a horse can start to get mean, even though that isn't what he wants to do.

The horse may not be doing the "right" thing for what the rider is asking of him; but as far as the horse is concerned, *in his mind*, the horse *is* doing the right thing, from where he is.

The reason the horse may put so much resistance in there could be because the person has missed on the punishment part. I don't like to think punishment is the answer—I think directing and support is. These are real important factors to try to bring out, so that people will *think*.

When a person is learning, he may think he knows pretty well where he is, and that he is doing all right; but there's still that possibility of a doubt. Maybe he does the right thing at the right time. Maybe that's all he can do, but the horse doesn't understand, or maybe the horse doesn't respond just right at that time.

If people can understand the importance of *communication*, then they won't get disturbed, but if they miss this, then it isn't so easy.

I think all of us get bothered inside at times. If the inside of a person or a horse is bothered, it's for sure that the outside is going to show it. There is so much variation in what's going on in the inside of that horse that is telling you where the troubled spot is. (I used to include this part in the mental part as well as the physical part, you see.) You need to learn about what's going on inside the horse. But, the inside of that horse is right in his innards, you might say; and what brings on trouble is disturbance, both mental and physical, being brought to the inside of the horse—right in his innards. If you can feel this, it will tell you a lot about what's causing his trouble.

I didn't used to elaborate on the third factor, spirit; I only just mentioned it. But I've begun to wonder about it in the last few years. Maybe if people got to realizing the importance of that part of the horse, they could get more feel and understanding from right in the horse's innards. Then they could try to figure out the mental and the physical parts.

I've felt this in horses all my life, but I don't think I realized how important it was to try to calm that inward part down. I was always working on the surface, both mentally and physically—not getting right down to the inside of the horse. No one is going to get this without it coming right out of the inside of themselves. The rest of it has to come from inside the horse. Mind, body and spirit is what we are talking about here.

I have helped riders who thought they had a horse problem, but I tell them the horse is having a "people problem." These riders don't seem to realize that the horse thinks he is supposed to do just what he is doing; even though the horse doesn't know why or what it is for. He is sure he is *supposed* to do it and does all he possibly can to do it.

When this is happening, often the rider feels just as sure that the horse is doing what he is doing because he doesn't want to do what the rider is asking. The rider may completely miss that the horse is doing just what he has been trained to do.

With anyone who has had some success, whether it is in everyday work or in the show ring, there are a few things that work—that fit well. They hit in those things; but there are all these other opportunities, all around, that they don't seem to realize exist. They try to get these high spots to carry them over the weak spots, and they just kind of "fill in" everywhere else.

I don't know anything about music, but years ago someone was talking about the difference between a person who learned to play by note and one who learned to play by ear. If a person learned to play by note, he could keep building on what he had learned. The person who had learned just by ear could do a lot, but so many of them would hit on some good notes, then just fill in a little on something. Then they would hit some more good notes. It wasn't too bad, a lot of it; but it wasn't something they could really build on. I've thought of that a lot of times with some people and their horses. They have a few good spots and instead of branching out to get some more to go with it, they just head for those high spots (the notes they know) and don't realize there are a whole bunch more of them just as important as the ones they have found that work for them. Sometimes there can be some dandy spots, but in between there are all those flat spots and sour notes.

People will, I'm pretty sure, recognize when something fits, and when it doesn't fit they recognize it, but often they haven't been able to separate and identify what is taking place between the two. What doesn't fit often just gets blamed on the horse. They think he is not cooperating.

People need to realize that there is a big responsibility there for the person. The rider can be really sincere and try his best, but if he doesn't have that picture it doesn't matter how sincere he is. He can miss a lot.

The rider can miss the fact that he has trained the horse to do what he is doing. The rider can be thinking of it as a takeover, while the horse can be thinking he is doing OK. When the horse gets into those spots he just tries to live through it the best he can—he just kind of shuts everything off.

Sometimes the riders will be so anxious to get going from where they are now to where they would like to be. Many times there isn't a way of answering what they are asking without taking in the surroundings that go with it. If I could get everything to fit the question, that would be great, but when all these other things feed into that question, any one or a combination of them can throw the whole thing clear out of balance.

Riders may want to get an answer to their questions right early—on the surface. I want them to try to *figure out* something; I want them to work at figuring out the whole horse—his mind, body and spirit. Maybe they will figure out what they are missing.

Responsive and Right On

If I could tell people, just go through the motions here, and then they could pick this up and do it, I wouldn't do anything else but work with people and horses; but I can't do that. There is something more. It is something that has to come in the unity between the horse and the rider. And there is a delicate line that makes the difference.

The rider can be missing by just so little, but it makes a big difference to the horse. I've tried everything! Forty years ago I thought I was going to find a way people could just pick this up. The riders can be using it some, but they don't have that feel and timing refined enough to where they can tune the thing up. For years I have struggled to analyze this so people could understand, to bring it out loud and clear, to have it be effective for the rider. The horse and the rider can be right there, both good, and I can be doing all I can to help get this thing to operate, and it still isn't easy for the person. Most people do not recognize how delicate it is.

The thing that I am trying to bring out here is this feel and timing. I used to say all there is to it is feel, timing and balance. I still can't improve on those three words, but there is so much that goes on within that.

Some riders I have worked with are getting closer and closer to feeling the feet, and where they are, and what is going to happen before it even happens. If the horse is needing a little support, a little directing, a little help, they are more ready to help the horse at the time the horse needs it. If the horse is going to make it anyway, these riders don't get in the way, and that is *so* important. Then these riders will get so they can *feel the whole horse*, what's going on all through the horse, one part complementing the other. Until that is working, the rider is at the mercy of a lot of things. A rider can be so close, he might just as well have it working.

I don't know just how to go about getting these things across. I used to say, "If I could just crawl inside your hide for just five minutes then you could do it." But I don't know. It's all there, but is hard for a person to recognize. It's experience I guess.

What I am trying to help the rider experience is what you need before you ever get on your first horse. But *if you ever get it*, it comes later!

I am trying to help the horse every bit I can to learn to come through so that he will be able to get himself together. It is the first thing I start to help a horse to do. Even if it is a horse that has been ridden more and gotten calloused, hard spots, I still try to get him to understand, but it takes so much more time and work, for both the horse and the person.

I don't know any other way to get this, so a rider feels it, except by starting from scratch. A rider can be struggling for it; he knows it can be, but just how to get it to work is the problem.

I have spent hours with the horse and rider trying to help the rider experience unity between the horse and himself. What I want is for the rider to try to reach for the horse, just as if they were going to start forward. It's important to remember to keep the head and neck centered. If the horse backs up a step or two, it's all right, just so he stays straight.

If the horse doesn't feel like he is quite all together, that's OK, as long as the rider keeps track of what happens. It may take quite a while for *the horse to get just right on.*

At the time the rider has the contact, when the horse gets himself together and right on—center—then he can come forward. He will be even, *in balance.*

The rider will be watching so the horse doesn't leave too early, just trying to steady the horse a little until he gets all together. The horse can be so close, he is all around it. Sometimes a rider can be so close he knows when it happened, but not recognize it. If it does come through, the rider may not really feel the whole thing take shape. There is a spot where they don't really have it all together. This is the spot we are trying to get close to, so the rider can feel when it isn't there, and be able to feel where the horse needs a little help, a little directing and support and when it is time to just *let it happen.*

When you get tired you can do something else, because being confined too long on something isn't good either. You need variety for the person, just the same as for the horse.

At first the horse doesn't know how to get this all together; but once it gets to working, the horse likes it just as much as the rider.

This is going right back to the beginning, as much as I can get it to be. But once the horse catches up on it, and you get to the point where you can help him know what you are asking, *then* you can get on him and this will just come, and you can be right off at the canter, or he could be running, and you wouldn't lose this good feel. *This is what could be.*

The rider needs to get to the point where he realizes how important the hind quarters are; if they aren't working just right, he may notice it more in the front end, but they both have to work, and each one has to complement the other. The problem may show to the rider more in front. It seems to appear that way to most people. It is important to get caught up on this or the rider may not get it.

A horse can be almost caught up, but still leave a little early, *just an instant.* Had he waited just that instant, he would have been all together. You may let him work at it. He will start to hunt. He can be a little out of time in front when he isn't hunting in the back quarters enough. Let him hunt there for a while to where, when you ask him, he will start preparing back there. Then you can feel the life come through. You can see it shaping up. The horse fills right in and he can come on through.

This is the goal: when you reach, or you let him know, he shapes up and the whole horse is all together—balanced. It seems to me, until a person gets this, he is going to be struggling with a lot of things. This is basic.

Pretty soon you just reach for the horse and he comes forward for you, right on—later you just reach for him—he comes and you can go forward or back.

The rider will wait for the horse to get balanced. He may be getting alive but not be getting his body weight balanced, to where if he started, the one end would be ready to complement the other. You want them to move off free. If you have them under too much, or if they are out too much, it seems as if it is hard for them to balance themselves, to position—so they can balance themselves right, to get the weight off the foot they need to move, to get the first step.

When you are trying to help the horse learn how to get started, do anything you can to help him try to get in a position that will help him get the rest of himself together—body, feet and legs—so that he can shift his weight in order to move the proper foot—or proper feet—at the proper time.

You'll find a place that fits the horse. It will vary on different individuals. As they get more advanced, they know how to position for different things. You get the horses so they will come through, regardless, so that any place you reach for them, this *good feel* comes. That helps them shift their weight for the different transitions. They learn to shift their weight so they can place their feet, so they are balanced. You try to help them as little as possible, but sometimes that is everything you have; or the other extreme, so little it's hardly measurable.

When it comes to where the horse is going to do it, then you leave as much up to him as you possibly can, *so that he will do it.* You are still supporting and directing, but you don't have to do much once he gets to operating.

Some people feel the rider makes a mistake when the pressure isn't released *after* the horse comes through. It is released when the horse is going to yield—that is the time when you ease the pressure, *before* it happens. *If you see that it is going to happen,* I'd say you withdraw your pressure *before* it happens, because if he is starting to do it, and the pressure is still there, it's in the way of the horse. He is trying to use his own mind and body to do this, and if the person won't allow that to happen, he interferes with the process.

This is one of the places that a person gets to a certain point where he can do quite a little without any of those finer things. But the more advanced he gets, then these little things make more difference on what the end results will be. When the horse is needing to figure out just when and how much, and a person doesn't allow him to use his own mind and body for that, he can't do his best. You have to encourage some horses and maybe support and direct them more than others.

Trying to help the horse find it, *the easiest for the horse*, and with the least effort for the person and the horse, is the thing that you try to keep in mind.

When you put the horse first and try to work from where the horse is, back to the person, it makes it easier for the horse to find. I'd say most people start from where the person is and try to get the horse to work back to them. All the time, the horse is trying to tell you where he is. Listen to the horse. Try to find out what the horse is trying to tell you.

Now when the whole horse is together, he will feel good to you, I am sure. All we are trying to do is fix these things up to where he can find them; then it's the horse's idea. *But that is a little easier said than done.*

When the horse is standing, before you reach to ask him to go forward or back, or turn right or left; *before you ask him*, have a picture in your mind of what you are going to ask him to do, and how you expect him to respond—*before you start*. Sometimes a rider will feel the horse walking right into the bit and pushing; instead of yielding through to the feet, he may take ahold of the bit at each corner, one and then the other, before he starts to give a step. A horse can be where a lot of good is shaping up, but he may still have those little quirks he doesn't need. These little "quirks" need to fade right out of the picture. When you reach for him he will get in the right position and frame of mind. The rider can be missing in the approach. It is the approach you take that brings out the life and good form.

When the rider reaches, the horse may be alive, but instead of waiting to find out which direction the rider is asking to go, the horse makes the selection. Instead of the rider selecting, the horse may not wait to find out which way the rider was going to ask him to go. He may just get the life and go forward. Earlier I said, before you reach, have it in your mind; picture which way you are going to ask the horse to go.

You can feel the life when you start to reach; you can feel that life come and his back elevating right under the saddle. You can feel it *all* shaping up. What the horse is doing, when the life is through the whole horse and the *message is to his feet*, is raising his back so he can get his feet free. He will raise his back and tip his weight off the foot he needs to move.

The horse will need to learn to separate the signals. When you ask him, he starts to get the life in his feet. First the rider needs to get the horse to *thinking* about backing, and then the horse will start to bring life right to those feet when the rider starts to ask him.

In starting this work, sometimes it will take just a few minutes to get this message through to the feet. Some horses will have a tendency to want to go forward just a little instead of preparing to go back. At the time when the horse needs to start preparing to position to back, he may start forward. If so, he walks into pressure and then gets ahold and pushes—if that happens you won't try to move his feet. As the horse goes up into *his* pressure that he's putting on himself, the rider will just wait and the horse will move his feet away from his own pressure. *Don't be in a hurry*. You let the horse move his feet. You wait for his feet to move; don't try to move them. The horse will do that.

To start with, the horse may yield to his own pressure, but be teetering. Then when he starts to get right on, straight and even, where it means something to him, the rider will be smooth and easy with him. But remember the horse puts the pressure on himself; he'll move away from his own pressure. Let him apply the pressure so that, in his mind, he is putting it on himself. If you present this to them as if they are putting the pressure on themselves, then they will yield to their own pressure to freedom. If the rider can get that separated for himself and the horse, then things will be easy and that heaviness will disappear.

It is easy for horses to understand it pretty early; if it is presented to them so they are the ones the pressure is coming from, it's their pressure, not yours.

Years ago, when I first became aware of this, sometimes something seemed to be shaping up pretty good, because sometimes it would happen pretty good. Other times not so good, and a person has a tendency to blame the horse when it isn't working out right.

Occasionally I would find out how to prevent these undesirable things from happening. In maybe one instance or one situation, things would seem pretty good. But then there would be something else. Some of those things a person doesn't think too much about; you just kind of live with them until you discover some time later that it doesn't have to be that way. That is probably when I began to realize the importance of trying to figure out what takes place when something is working pretty good, what caused it to come out that way. Or if something is not working so well, you compare the two.

This is where I began to realize that straightness in a horse is one of the most important things to keep in mind, right from the time you start riding him. The horse doesn't have to be straight, especially the first ride. The rider needs to be aware of the importance of where the horse is going to need the help, in order to learn to develop straightness, instead of just going along until something gets established and it gets in the way. As you try to progress, as the horse advances, one side is maybe better than the other. If the person hasn't been aware of this all along until this gets set, it's more difficult for the horse and person to try to figure it out and *overcome it.*

I'm quite sure a lot of people don't give that much thought. They feel there is a difference there, but they just kind of live along with it, then they try to do something about it. Sometimes if the horse is straight, it may not even feel right to the person, because he is so used to the horse going crooked. Actually, I think, that is the most important of all to understand. Yet, so many times what a person is doing to try to correct it is just the opposite of what the horse needs.

From then on it is a matter of learning the importance of the body's balance. I began to recognize the feel of the horse when I began to realize the importance of working with that body balance. All these other things, like the position that the horse would be in when he felt good or the position he would be in when he didn't feel good, I was aware of, but it seemed as if it wasn't as easy to overcome the undesirable without maybe getting in the way of the more desirable things.

After I got to thinking about things more, I realized you didn't have to have a horse there to figure out a lot of these things. You could go to bed at night and think it over and figure out what approach you might need to take the next day. You have a chance then to figure out where the horse is and what you need to do to help the horse catch up on things he needs.

Until a person starts to develop that ability to figure things out in himself, he can work until doomsday and there will be times when things happen to work out pretty good for him, but until he actually understands what ticks, he is going to have problems. The horse is liable to be the one that has the first problem and then the person from there.

When I am trying to put it into words and am right there where the horse can respond, and the person still doesn't get it, it's pretty hard to think of words that will take care of it in a book.

Trying to find fitting words that are understandable and effective for a person to get these ideas--to know when each thing is fitting, so that the person can try to apply it at a time when it is the easiest for the horse to understand and get things separated—is a slow process.

In working with people I find they get so they do enough so that it seems that it's starting to be effective and understood, but it isn't too long until they are right back doing the same things they were before. That's another one of the difficult spots.

For instance, one of the things I often think about is just doing up the latigo—like raising that rigging up and poking the latigo up from the underside. Many people go over the top, and it will work either way, but the more convenient way when you go to put the saddle on, and cinch again, is for the latigo to be tucked up from the underside—it just feeds out easy. If it weren't for the ease feature it wouldn't matter—if the rider doesn't want to do it that way it still doesn't matter. A lot of people I've worked with have seen that and thought, "Well, that's pretty good"; they practice a little and think it works better. But the next time I'd see them they would be doing the latigo from the top again. They didn't even realize they were still not doing it the way that they thought was the good deal. It seemed like they were just unaware; they went right back in their same track. It really didn't matter—they were still getting the saddle on, and cinched up, but they weren't getting any value out of the idea.

That is very similar to a lot of these other things, like getting on. Any horse that I have come across so far can learn to stay put, to allow a rider to get on, but if a person is just doing it without thinking about it and taking care of that, the horse isn't going to either stand or be dependable in different situations. He may stand part of the time and other times he won't. If the person is thinking of that and the approach he takes is fitting, that horse will stand there regardless. If it isn't that important to the person to try to get that established, it really doesn't matter.

A lot of people think they would like to have everything working well, but if it's going to be that much trouble, they decide they don't need it. This is the attitude they get especially if they have worked at it for a while and then realized it was important to think on it. When things aren't shaping up, if the riders would just stop—I don't mean they have to stop what they are doing, but if they would just *stop* and *think*—they can still be going ahead. I guess I'm trying to say *stop their thinking* and take a fresh start. They seem to feel that they *are* thinking, but maybe there's something else that needs to be mentioned along with that. Some of their thinking could be more effective on what they may need to figure out. Probably understanding what to look for, or what the need is, would be the first important thing to try to understand. People can give all their attention, do everything they possibly can, seemingly, in trying to be cooperative, but maybe the problem is in their understanding of the horse; or in understanding what they themselves need to recognize and realize.

In cattle work, occasionally somebody mentions that if he starts toward the herd, his horse, instead of hooking on and going there, is maybe thinking more of avoiding that direction, instead of just going there and understanding that was where the horse and rider were going and it could be something the horse was interested in and could enjoy. In visiting with some people about that, I find they themselves were feeling just like the horse. Once they get about so near the herd, the horse seems to get a little more eager; he wants to get in there and work and get it over with. Then when they finish working, the horse wants to get back. Well, quite a bit of that, I believe, is just the way the *person* is feeling. If the person was enjoying it or understood a little more about it, so it could be a little more pleasant and interesting, then maybe the horse would feel different about it too. I don't believe people realize how important that is to the horse.

Sometimes I've seen kids in jumping lessons. The jump was maybe just a little higher than the rider felt comfortable with, but he still thought he had to take it or thought he wanted to take it (inside, he was not too sure). Sometimes those old horses just wouldn't take that jump. They were trying to protect the kid, or reacting to the feel of the kid. It's kind of like a person could say, "I want to do that," and "I don't want to do that." Some of these things, I think, really happen a lot more than most of us realize.

The other extreme would be a person asking for something beyond what he can handle and the horse can handle, just because he thinks somebody else is doing it, and he should try it. If it works, fine, but if it doesn't work he really has nothing to draw on for support for himself and the horse. One person can develop the ability, but with another it just seems to have its limitations. That all has to be taken into consideration. A person has to understand himself, his limitations, along with the horse, and then try to get the two to blend. Just because someone seems to be getting something worked out pretty well, another person could try to do the same thing, and it wouldn't work at all, because he wouldn't be prepared for it.

He would, maybe, have to take years before he could get up to that. If he understood this and worked on it, and also recognized his limitations and still understood how to try to prevent the horse from getting beyond where the rider could operate, it would be helpful.

In most cases people are not going to go to extremes. They are going to try to find a horse they can get along with, or quit riding and do something else. There are instances where people have the ability and desire; they are interested and could put this to use and it would have a lot of value for them. The horse may be bothered, but be good to work with because he is so alive, has tremendous feel and really wants to be all right.

To understand what is taking place, people need to picture what is taking place and then be able to get themselves into the picture. What seems to be missed is how the person can make those adjustments. First they have to, you might say, pinpoint the area or areas where this picturing is needed in order for the rider to help the horse either overcome or find these things. For instance, I will say, "We'll compare the two sides, then that gives us a chance to help the horse do better on the side that is not so good without taking away any of the good part from the good side." Sometimes, it is a difference in that whole side, and sometimes it is just in the shoulder, or the neck, or along the ribs, or anywhere in the rear quarters. When they start searching for these things they may only recognize it on one area; or it might feel like the whole thing is all the same, when there is actually quite a variation all the way through. Until the rider gets to thinking of all those things and feeling and listening to the horse, the rider is going to go out there and try to just "do an action" and make it happen instead of trying to see, feel and sort it out.

Then the timing that you ask for might not fit—then too, you can ask for it in the right way and at the right time, but it may not mean very much to the horse right at that time. You may have to do other things for a while that may be almost completely opposite—clear away from it, and then come back. Sometimes you'll work these other things all around with the hope the horse will discover what it is needing without getting him in over his head—getting him stuck and uninterested. The thing that is so important is the desire—to try to hold that desire—to develop it, if it isn't there—or if you have more desire than is fitting then you'll work other things in to try to keep the horse occupied while you are trying to help him hit on this spot where he needs to come through.

In the "feedback" section of this book, there is enough similarity that the reader can kind of get the idea of how it can be; still it is hard to describe and hard to understand. There is still enough variation so that while one person may dwell on one subject and someone else on another one, the variety could help. In the overall there is an area there where they know what can be, but they can't quite describe it.

Maybe some of these points we are trying to bring out in this book can bring something to the surface the reader had very little understanding of; or hadn't even thought about before—things they may have been bypassing. If some of these ideas will bring them to the surface, then maybe there will be a way of digesting it.

Sometimes you get a little interest aroused; but even when you get that interest working some there has to be understanding for it to operate, in order for much advantage to come of it; otherwise the interest will either get to wandering, or get lost—*get scattered without some understanding blending in with it.*

You might get some understanding operating in order to increase the interest, too. It could be a little one way at different times for different things that are being worked on. These are all things I don't know quite how to bring to life for a book. It's hard for a person to get that broad coverage of the way it could be so that people could be seeing it, feeling it, or picturing it.

Approach and Unity
(Another Grain)

I once heard a tale about a king who liked stories and wanted a story that would never end. The king had a slave and he declared the slave could live if he would agree to tell him a story that never ended. So the slave told the king about a granary full of grain and a locust came and got a grain of wheat; then another locust came and got a grain of wheat, and so on. Finally the king didn't want any more. He felt as if he'd have to kill the slave if the story didn't stop. This could be a little like what could happen in some parts of this work. I hope before the urge to murder strikes, the reader will recognize just the right grain to fit his need.

In the feedback section, the examples sometimes seem almost the same, but if it's coming from different individuals, it may fit different riders, and somebody will start picking something up. In different individuals, a lot of things are kind of uniform, but there is actually a variation in there; and that variation is when a person really wants to do some thinking. It isn't the intention of this book to be a "how to do" book. It is meant to show different experiences so people may figure out how they can get it done, instead of "you do this and you get that."

I never did a whole lot of reading. Quite a few of these things I just finally stumbled on to; it seemed like some of these things got to working for me and then in reading, some of the things I had experienced were verified.

At one time when I read something in a book I would think, "Maybe this will tell the whole thing—will *have the answer*." But it doesn't work like that. Writers have real good intentions, but one individual might get quite a bit out of the book and another reader might not get anything. Then, too, there might not be a lot you understand the first time you read something, but after you have read it and then worked at it, after a while you may understand more.

There is so much variation in the human individual that the approach has to be a little different in order to fit each person. They might come out with the same results as someone else, but if everyone tried to take the same approach, there wouldn't be too many of them coming out with the same solution. That's another thing I think is important to emphasize—*this is an individual process.* I tell people that over and over when they are trying to get something worked out. I say, "All I can do is try to help." It has to come right out of the inside of the individual. There's no other way I know of that they can get it. It depends on what the situation may be; there might be many things, but there is variation in how they are applied. People tend to say, "That's a little deep; I know what you are saying but I don't understand it."

Another spot is if you are working with a horse that doesn't know what you are asking it to do. With horses you have to get their respect before you will get a response. With other horses, you will try to get a response in order to get their respect. Respect and response can be closely associated, but they can also be quite a distance apart at different times, maybe even in the same horse you are working with at different stages of the process.

The approach and unity between the horse and the person needs to be emphasized. Included in this is the approach that the person takes— and the horse's approach from where it is, too. As you are approaching, the horse could be a little bothered; you try to regulate that, you ease off a little to where the horse can accept it. It may be just on a teeter, until the horse finds out it's OK. For a lot of people, when I say approach and unity, that doesn't mean anything. It isn't understood, but it's real important to the horse, especially when catching a horse or working with colts.

On the baby foals, the older I get the earlier I like to get them to handling, because the baby foals are just as quick as they were fifty years ago, but I'm not nearly as quick as I was twenty years ago. So in order to try to not get myself in too deep—before the foals get heavier—I like to start working with them. They may squirm around just as much when they are a week old as they would when they are six months old, but there's not that weight. I can't handle that like I might have at one time. As I got older I found out these young ones learn just as fast, or maybe faster, than the older ones. It's surprising how quick these little ones catch on and how lasting it is. This is where getting older has helped me find out some things that I might not have thought of if I had been younger. Again, I have had to adjust to a situation that best fits the occasion from my standpoint.

My approach is not quite so sudden, and there is a time and a waiting for the foal to present itself to me more than me presenting myself to it. The foals are not so likely to squirm as much.

Most foals have a lot of curiosity. Some of them are extremely strong that way. As I've gotten older I've watched more for that and let them apply more of what's coming from them to me. I encourage that

Tom making young friends in June 1987 at Merced, California

to where they do a lot of filling in that I used to try to do for them. After they have presented that curiosity and they have an opportunity to put it to use, then I try to think more of directing so that I am developing respect and response and it's coming from them. There isn't nearly as much squirming that takes place now as it might have at one time. There is not nearly as much squirm in me and it's keeping the foals from being so squirmy. That's where the learning process from the foal is becoming effective—more effective than it ever was; the respect is easier to blend in with the response.

A baby foal can soon get obnoxious without some direction; with some direction they can let all that is good in them have an outlet in a useful directing way; they are much happier about it. They seem to feel much more secure. They respect that. A lot of times people say it's better not to touch a foal until the person is ready to go on with it, and if the person misses on this part, they'd better leave it alone, because they will have a mess. It's so important and yet almost dangerous. It's a delicate situation.

When I'm working with a foal, I try to keep things interesting enough for it, but anytime the foal gets a little unsure and wants to withdraw I back up and take a fresh start; maybe then, or some other day.

I try to leave them with the impression that they are always welcome. So many times people miss that. They get them caught but there's a spot there that makes quite a difference: the approach and the understanding of their natural self-preservation. Really, all horses have this. It's strong in the young ones—that's their built-in security—self-preservation. They haven't had bad experiences; they just have natural caution. It's when they have some bad experiences, along with their natural self-preservation protection, that it takes more understanding from the person to get the horse's confidence back.

On these young ones, if they get confidence in the person and themselves, then all a person has to do is watch that he doesn't destroy it. You will expose them to experiences, and the horse will be able to separate and experience from the exposure and from you. You will be careful that you don't upset the self-preservation; they measure and they evaluate. The horse can do so many things then by being aware of how far he can carry himself on into situations and still be safe. That's a spot that I often mention, where you try to help the horse get to where he feels like you could ride him up a telephone pole or down a badger hole; *you won't do either one but they feel like you could.*

It's amazing what a horse will be able to tolerate if he understands it's all right. It's like in this petting and scratching; you can dig right in on him once he gets to going along with it. To start with, if he doesn't understand that it is going to be all right he couldn't even stay close. It would scare him and he wouldn't feel secure. It seems like riders don't realize how much they can build this in, security and the acceptance of different experiences.

People are working with security and acceptance all along as they are riding these horses, preparing them for different uses, but I don't know as they give that enough thought, how important the initial approach is and getting the horse to approach them with the understanding that it is all right. There may be some uncomfortable things there, but they still understand that it is fitting because the horses understand what is taking place, or they take an interest in the work that is being done.

Yesterday I rode a four-year-old stallion for the first time in about about a week. Before, I had been getting him so I could ride him around the other horses, but still if I came by where these other horses were, he would still like to stop; but today we could go right on. Soon he could take in the surroundings and still do the work—the same thing with the calves—he could be following one of them or working one of them right where these other horses were, and he could take care of the work and take in the surroundings at the same time. It even made things better and more interesting for him. A couple of the fillies were in heat, and I was trying to help him in the handling, so that he wouldn't try to leave what we were doing in order to go socializing. I made use of that opportunity to help him develop going where I would direct, or have a place to head for. He would still know where I was trying to hook him on to; he would still know where he was going.

First I worked at a distance so that if he started to take over I'd have room to get him to drift—carry on—or if he tried to take over I'd have room for recovery, be able to stay out of the corner. First I would have to go kind of sideways—drift along when these things happened. Then later he could go straighter. Even later I could reach over the fence and ride along and pet or scratch the horses and he would just go along with me. I had to watch, but he could do that. I was trying to see how little it took, to see if I could leave the reins free. He is just getting to where you can go a ways free and then he has to check it out again.

When I started riding him I'd go out through the pasture where there were two fillies and a gelding. He would let them come up and sniff him through the fence. I'd keep his rear quarters to where they could touch him, maybe nibble on him a little, and if it got to where they were overdoing it, we would just move on a little ways. That is where it started; now we are able to ride in the same pasture. It's making quite a difference to him; it's getting those feet in your hands. It's good for him, and I can sit on him around there and it isn't too strenuous. I can do that and accomplish quite a little, whereas if I had to manhandle him I wouldn't make it.

I'm not doing much of anything anymore—I'm not talking a whole lot most of the time, except days like this—but on these little foals I've made a point to get them strong on the right hand side; then if they get lopsided, it's easier to get them back. When I used to start horses and someone else was going to be riding them after they were started, I'd try to get them so they were handier to the right hand side than they were to the left. Then if somebody started to ride them and they got handier to the left, it was easier to get balanced if I rode one again.

I have found as the years have gone by, the importance of helping the horses learn how to prepare to position so if they are straight they can go either way, take the left lead or the right lead. They don't have to be right on, but if they learn how, they would rather be. That's where the difference is. If it doesn't matter to the person it doesn't matter; but when they go to do something and the horse isn't positioned, it isn't going to be as easy, so then it's just drill, drill, drill, without helping the horse learn how to prepare to position for whatever the transition is. Occasionally you see a horse who operates a little better to the right than to the left, but generally they are better to the left.

It's a little hard for people to figure out sometimes what is right or left handed on a horse. If you start out following an animal out there and that animal bends to the left, I like for that horse to position himself so he can lead out with his left. Then if that animal crosses over and changes sides, he should reach on the right.

If you are going in a circle, he is on the inside either way, but if you are going down the fence, instead of having him on the inside lead, you had better have him on the outside lead, if you are going to turn and come back—when they come out of that bend they are reaching. Of course as he gets more seasoned, the horse gets so he plans ahead. Later he can be making a transition and positioning at the same time as he makes those sudden moves. If it is set up for the horse before he gets a set pattern it is much easier, even though he may be missing part of the time on the lead that is fitting. Instead of making a big issue of it, just try to arrange it so it just comes out to where it fits the horse—he will learn it and won't even know he has learned it—instead of going out to drill and drill.

Thirty or forty years ago, I just thought anybody that rode probably recognized these things. When I said, "If a horse doesn't feel right on one side, or as well on one side as the other, then compare the sides, try to figure out what is taking place on the side that seems to fit the best—then try to help the horse learn to position the other side." I thought that would be quite a benefit for people to try to really feel what was going on. As time went on, I began to realize that while I was talking about those things people were just waiting until I got through talking, so they could ask about something they were not ready for. Other times people will start to work on something and they may be working too hard, really. They are trying to get it all right away. Can't blame them for that, but it takes a while sometimes.

Along in the early '30s, I used to take a few horses to the county fair to race. They were just ranch horses, but the rest of the horses at the fair were also ranch horses.

Some of the kids around town would come down to the fairgrounds. I would usually put them to work doing something—leading a horse, or cleaning stalls, or something. One of these boys came out to the ranch the next summer after school was out. He was left handed and he wanted to learn how to rope. When I handed the boy a rope, he started to make the loop with his left hand. I told him it wasn't going to be any more difficult for him to learn to rope right handed than it would be left handed. After he got so he could throw the rope right handed, then he could learn left handed; that way he could use either hand. He had quite a struggle but he was an ambitious kid and pretty sharp too. He soon got handy with his right hand. He could throw that rope on a post or a calf. When I noticed he was doing pretty good on that, I said, "Now let's go back to your left." He had quite a struggle getting started with his left hand, but he got so he could do almost as well with his left as his right.

I have thought of that a lot of times. How similar it is with animals and people. Most riders, when they start out, go to the left. I try to get people to think about starting to the right hand direction so that the horse is going to get a little more exercise to the right than to the left. Most of them are already set to the left; then if you only have time to go one way you've already got your horses right hand side exercised. If you get a pattern you are liable to turn that same way over and over.

It looks good to me when the rider has enough working for him so he can feel when it's right and when it isn't—or when it's just not quite there—when they just keep fixing and waiting and it shapes up. Then it gets right on, the horse learns how to get right on, then stay put and carry. *The rider is feeling that horse and learning what is taking place from the horse.* The rider is starting to operate from where the horse is, and then trying to work the horse back to where the rider needs him and where the horse needs to be, instead of the rider trying to start from where he would like to have the horse. So many times people try to have the horse do just what they want, but the horse hasn't even gotten close to thinking of that. It takes a while for the horse to start thinking of that.

You have to feel and listen to what is taking place within the horse and if he feels like he's not going to shape up or going to position so that he can come through like you'd like for him to, you can help him get back on course.

You don't have to do these things in order to go along and do well and be successful—but only if you're interested. And sometimes it is more interesting and more rewarding, *especially for the horse.*

From Editor to Readers

Dear Readers,

Some of you have been waiting for this book for several years. Tom has worked personally with you and your horse. You have experienced and seen in action those moments when horse and rider are truly one. True unity is achieved, and it seems almost like "magic." Observers have even used the word "magic" to describe the moment, but the real excitement is in the joy of realizing these moments of completeness are not illusion. These moments are reality for the horse and rider to share. As the rider learns to recognize these moments the picture can develop from an illuminating snapshot to an art form in motion.

Probably not all of you who are reading this are riders, and not all riders picture themselves seriously striving to achieve riding as an art. But I believe riders and non-riders alike can visualize and learn to recognize and appreciate true unity between the horse and the rider.

For over twenty-six years I have witnessed the changes in and between horse and rider as Tom shared his knowledge and vision with them. As frustration and fear were replaced by knowledge and trust, as confusion became confidence, and discord became harmony, the picture of what "could be" came into focus.

The following "feedback" section includes responses from riders who have taken the time to share their feelings and experiences about working with Tom. These responses represent a wide range in age and a diversity in background. Some are from riders who have worked with Tom for years; others for only a season.

Each response shows a rider involved in his or her own struggle to bring into focus the picture of what "can be" between the horse and rider.

No doubt you, as a reader, will realize how difficult it is to picture on paper even a fraction of the complexity of this situation. The actions, reactions and interactions involved in one moment when horse and rider are in true harmony with one another could fill a volume to picture. The picture could still be out of focus for the rider until the instant that person experiences for himself the true unity that is possible between horse and rider.

This material has been prepared not to give you a "magic" formula but to share with you the assurance that these experiences of oneness are a reality for the horse and rider to share. These responses represent only a fraction of the riders involved in their search toward willing communication between the horse and the rider.

Thank you to all the people who have contributed to this section. You have been a big help and encouragement.

A special "Thanks" also to the people who helped by reading and critiquing portions of the book.

Milly Hunt Porter, editor

Respondents

Respondents' names are listed in alphabetical order, not in the order in which the responses appear.

Bob Barrett
Julia Batchez
Allie Bear
Martin Black
Mary Branscomb
Bob Carlson
Lynette Culbert
John DeLong
Bill Dorrance
Ellen Eckstein
Kent Heneks
Jeanette Hogan
Martha Hogan

Randy Leighton
Tom Marvel
Joyce Mattos
Sam Meads
Susie Mitchell
Mary Moiso
Sam Mori
Bryan Neubert
Daphne Raitt
Bill Van Norman
Charles Van Norman
Joe Wolters

Tom's Students Visit about Tom

I'll start where I started with Tom, when I first worked with Tom about fourteen years ago. The first time I started realizing what Tom was about, I had been here a couple of months and we were fixing something on the ceiling. Tom was on a short ladder and he needed a hammer. I was holding the ladder—and obviously it was a lot easier for me to go get the hammer. Tom said, "If I had a hammer I'd nail this up." I went and got it, but on the way over I was thinking to myself, "Why didn't he say will you please *go get* me a hammer?" But he said, "If I had a hammer I'd nail this board up." That was when I learned he was making it my idea. So I went for the hammer like a puppy chasing a stick. I ran over and grabbed it because I already knew what to do. That was when I first got on to Tom. He was like that all the time.

The year I worked with him at the ranch we didn't work with horses too much. At first I was really disappointed because we didn't, but then I found out later it wouldn't have mattered what we worked on. If we had been auto mechanics the whole time I would have learned just about as much anyway. That is just the way Tom is.

Another example of Tom with me—you know, he kind of worked along with me the way he would work with a horse or anything else. He taught me how to run a bulldozer. Most people wouldn't ever realize it—Tom is about one of the handiest catskinners there ever was. He can make a bulldozer do anything—it's unbelievable. So—he taught me how to run a bulldozer. He showed me the basics. He would say, "Well, I'll show you just enough so you can get into trouble, then I'll get out of your hair here." He'd show me just what to do and tell me what job he expected to be done; then he'd leave and be gone. He'd come back about a half hour or an hour later and say, "Well, how you doing?" I'd tell him how I was doing and he'd say, "Well, maybe if you were doing this a little different . . . " and he'd just make it real easy. I've seen so many guys trying to teach somebody to run a piece of equipment and they stand there and give directions. They are standing there and pointing and telling you what to do, and you can't even do it.

That's how Tom is with people and horses and that was when I started learning that Tom's way of thinking with the horses was by leaving them alone like that and letting them find it. Then he came back to it when I needed some help and some guidance and would show me—but never the pressure. So that was another example I realized about five years later.

When I first went to work there I told Tom, I said, "I understand you're pretty good with horses and I'm sure looking forward to working on these colts and getting some help on these horses with you." He said, "Well, I didn't think you needed any help really." I thought, "Man, I must really be doing good."

Then a week or so later I brought it up again. I said, "I'd sure like to start some colts." There were some colts there to be started. "I'd really like to get some help on these horses," I said. Tom said, "You just go along the way you are going. There are no serious problems right now. You just go along the way you are going and when something comes up that you need to work on, then we'll work on it." That was a big lesson for me because I thought I'd go there and Tom would just make a real horse breaker out of me—make a real hand out of me, but that wasn't the way it was; but I had to find that out, too.

When we did start working on horses, that was one of the problems. I started a colt there and I didn't really have near enough of the feel of that horse.

Tom was trying to get it across to me, but I wasn't really getting it, and he was having troubles trying to get me to get it. So, what he had me do was ride the horse in a straight line; but I was getting confused someplace. I don't remember now the specifics, but he just had me close my eyes. It was by the barn and it was a tin barn, and when I rode right by the end of the barn there was a little noise on the door that would make the horse kinda change directions. So, he had me close my eyes and ride back and forth by there for a half an hour; back and forth with my eyes closed. That's when he talked about riding a horse between your legs. He could take something that I'd try to make a big deal out of and I'd go on with ten steps of how to correct whatever the problem was. Then he'd take and break it down without me even realizing it—at the time he'd just be working at what my problem was. A lot of times I didn't realize these things until the next day—or maybe a month later—or a year later. When that problem came up sometime down the road it would dawn on me what Tom had meant.

Every day there is something I remember from watching Tom's horses. He rode the same horses I rode there. Some of them I didn't ride while he was there and he was riding them. I rode them after he left. Horses that he rode were all just ranch horses that other people had ridden there. I remember how all the horses were kind of cranky and switch-tailed. They were horses that their tendency was more that way anyway, naturally, more than some other horses. I'd ride them and get along with them, but I didn't really know, you know, wasn't really aware of what was going on. Then I'd watch Tom ride them and they would look like, "Well, where we goin' now—what's our job today? I can't wait to go out and do what we gotta do!"

I will never forget this one mare Tom was riding. He told me about the fellow who rode her before and all the problems that fellow had with this mare. She had gotten real bad to get along with. Just real bad coming home, getting hepped up. So, Tom started riding her and that was just about the time I went to work there. We'd be out riding; sometimes we would only ride once or twice in a week. Once after he'd ridden her three or four times, we'd been gone most of the day and it was a long ride home. It was getting late and he had been working on me getting my horse to walk out because he had to keep looking over his neck.

Of course I didn't know about staying with my horse and keeping it alive. So he was telling me, "You know, my neck gets kinda sore. That horse can walk as fast as any horse on this ranch so why don't you keep your horse up here with mine?" And he worked on me where I could stay beside him. It was fine; we got to going on that. Then we were heading on home—he was on this mare that would just never walk. We were going home and I'd been watching him work with her but I didn't understand anything that was taking place. It looked pretty confusing. I wasn't far enough along to appreciate how his timing was and what he was doing.

That night as we were coming home the sun was just setting. Riding in, that mare was walking so fast and her ears were just straight up, head down and those rein chains were just swaying back and forth. Tom had a smile on his face. He just sat there, reins draped over the horn and his arms folded. He said, "Yah! This is the way I like a horse to walk home." And I hadn't even realized he'd been working on getting that mare to walk—and then all of a sudden he has the reins draped over the saddle horn and his arms are folded. That's what Tom was to me, or is to me.

The last clinic we went to (in December of 1983) I hadn't seen Tom for quite a few years to work with him. I'd been getting some help from Bill on horses and Joe Walters and some other guys; but I hadn't been making a lot of progress and I hadn't been riding a whole lot of different colts so I had been kind of at a stand still.

This last clinic, the bay horse I was riding came from Nevada and he'd been used just strictly as a ranch horse and never had any time spent with him other than that. He was pretty bad to kick and scared of everything and real snorty. Every time you'd go to catch him he was one of those real snorty colts. I took him to the clinic to work on some other things, and Tom saw these things. Of course I thought, "Well, I don't want to work on these now. I want to take care of these more important things."

Tom didn't even want to hear about those other things because he knew I would take care of some of these things later anyway. I didn't even realize that, that weekend at the clinic, but I realized it about a week later when I went to catch that horse again. I walked right up to him and he just stood there. He had always snorted—he didn't snort. He didn't try to take off or anything. That was when I realized that all that horse needed was to be petted—to be reassured. I remembered how Tom, my whole weekend at the clinic, was making sure everyone petted my horse. Most horses I've just used, and there have been a few horses I've liked, but I really learned this last time to like all of them and to really be their friend. Now I make a point to show them some genuine affection. After all, they are doing a hell of a lot for me, you know. That made such a difference. I was telling Joe after the clinic, "You know, here I am supposed to be a big smart cowboy; worked with Tom for a year and getting all this help from all these other people and I had to pay fifty dollars to go to a clinic and learn how to pet my horse."

But it would have been worth $500 or $5,000, because that was the thing that horse had never gotten and it was the thing I was missing on. I wasn't abusing the horse; I was just trying to get along, but I didn't know how to take that extra step. I needed to make the extra step, not the horse.

There was something I meant to mention earlier, and I learned it on the bulldozer story. Tom said, "You'll get into positions where you'll just get real frustrated." (This was on the dozer piling a bunch of brush and I'd get in a jackpot looked like I'd never get out of it.) He'd say, "Looks like you're not going to get out of it; things will get real tough, then that's when you'll start getting mad and frustrated. That's the time. Don't let it get that far. Just stop. Shut the machine off, idle it down, park it, get off and go someplace. Go someplace for ten minutes. As soon as you start to get tired of it, go do something, even if it's just rest for ten minutes. Then come back to it and then it will be real easy."

Boy, I remembered that. I'd start having troubles on that machine — get frustrated and mad as hell and I'd remember what Tom said and I'd get off, then when I'd get back on it would seem like I'd been doing it all my life. It would come real easy then. And, of course, that's one of those things I learned on the bulldozer but didn't apply to the horses for a long time. Now, I'm just starting to remember to do that.

Since the last clinic I've been thinking a lot more of these things about letting the horse find it. A lot of times in order for me to let the horse find it I've got to back off, do something else, and come back to it because I get into too big a hurry and I try to make them find it.

I really realized this just the other day. I was at the Mountain House corrals and I had left two horses up there over the weekend and I took a two horse trailer up to haul them home. I thought there were halters up there but there weren't and I had no halters to move the horses into the trailer. They had only been in a two horse trailer a few times apiece anyway. They are not real easy loading. So, I thought, "Well, now what am I going to do? No halters."

It's a big corral about a hundred by a hundred feet. I knew the horses were ready to go home, so I just parked the trailer in the gate going home. I parked it so they could only get out of the corral one way—by going into the trailer. The one horse was the one I had at this last clinic. The other horse was Blackjack. All I had to do was get in the other end of the corral and start swinging my rope over my head a little bit, and they started trotting around looking for a way to go. Naturally they wanted to go over by that gate to go home; then they started finding themselves around the trailer. I'd start trying to get them to go in, then I would remember "*No, no, let them find it.*"

I just kept thinking to myself if Tom were sitting on the fence and he asked me to load them for him, how would I do it if he were sitting there. So, then I'd stop and wait—then I'd take a fresh start and I'd help them. I wouldn't wait for any major change—just the slightest change. That was something I had really missed on. After all these years I am really starting to realize it again. Just the slightest change—an ear wiggles a little bit one way—or the eye looks one way for just a split second—and that's all I had to look for. So, instead of trying to load the horses in a trailer I just tried to get them to think about looking that way. It took about thirty or forty minutes to load, because one horse was a lot more settled than the other one. One horse would pull out and one would stay there, and I was trying to make it difficult for the one horse and reward the other horse at the same time. That was the big challenge, having two horses that weren't very similar. But finally I got it working. The way I finally got it done—it got to the point where they were just ready to go in and I tried to press them too much. Then I had to stop—and that's when I was starting to get mad and think about getting them in there—then I thought about Tom for just a second. He just kinda crossed through my mind. He's like my conscience. I had Tom on my shoulder. So, when I have Tom on my shoulder I can get along with the horse—that sums it up, really.

If people take parts of it and misuse it—or make it less in other people's eyes—they are losing it anyway or they never got anything from it in the beginning. So, it's the people that get something out of it, what it all boils down to—all this is the twinkle in Tom's eye—that's what it boils down to.

One more little story I'm going to tell about Tom. When he was there at the ranch, we were putting in a tower for a TV antenna. We had to dig a hole in a mountain side in solid chalk rock. The hole had to be six feet deep by four feet square. It was a hell of a hole, in other words. We couldn't dig it with a shovel, and we didn't have the proper equipment. So, we did it with a digging bar and chipped away this hole, Tom and I. I was amazed at the stamina of this guy, anyway—working as hard as he did—and he's sore in the mornings and a little arthritic sometimes. He'd dig a few inches, and I would dig a few inches, and we'd trade off. We'd been working on this hole for two days, and we were finally getting down to the bottom. I was in there chipping the chips into a bucket, then he'd pull the bucket out and dump it; that's how slow a job it was.

We got almost all the way down to the bottom and we were looking at some cracks there in this chalk rock. If you are familiar with chalk rock, you know there are a lot of seams and cracks. We were way down there in the ground when we noticed some little hairs. They were root hairs; hairs that were growing off a root of an oak tree. The closest oak tree couldn't have been any closer than thirty or forty feet; but down in this little seam in these rocks were the hairs of the roots of an oak tree. Tom looked at these roots and said, "Boy! That's something, isn't it?" I wouldn't have given it much thought. He said, "These roots follow the path of least resistance." It was just a statement at that time, but in about five years I really realized how profound it was. At the time, I noticed how Tom is so aware of his surroundings and of everything that is. There we had been digging and sweating our brows for two days in these rocks, and he has the wherewithal after all this to notice a living root six feet down in the rocks and to notice that it takes the path of least resistance. Just like a colt will take the path of least resistance if you make the right thing easy and the wrong things difficult. It's the path of least resistance—people take the path of least resistance. If you're real friendly to people and make it easy for them to be with you—that's the least resistance and they'll be with you; but if you don't, then it's easier for them to go around, just like—to find that crevice in the rock. I think about that more and more all the time now.

After this last clinic, riding the different horses at home that I've been riding, I have found out something. I had one horse that I thought, "Well, he's OK but he's kinda dull." He wasn't as sensitive as some other horses. After the last clinic and really concentrating on giving the horses more time, and letting them find it—and letting them feel a good feel—I found out that that horse never had a chance to feel a good soft feel, and when he had felt it he hadn't felt it long enough to know that that is what we were both looking for. So, this one horse in particular has gotten a lot more sensitive—or he feels a lot more sensitive because I have allowed him to be that way. I thought it was because he was born that way, but it was because I had never offered that horse the good feel I've been trying to, but I had been missing it somewhere. That was another thing that came out of the last clinic.

— o —

There are so many things that Tom has taught me, that it is hard to express what these many experiences have done for my riding.

One particular phrase which Tom brings up frequently is "fix and wait." So often riders get in the way of the horse—trying to force what they want to happen. Tom has shown me that if you can learn to set up the situation so that the *horse* finds the easy way out then you have created a situation where the horse not only does what you want without resistance, but also *learns*. The few times that I have actually been able to do this is when I have experienced the "magic" that can exist in the relationship between the horse and rider. Those few moments where there is a true unity and a simple, willing communication as well as an enthusiastic cooperative attitude on the part of the horse. The theory seems so simple but it is so hard for people to put into practice because they refuse to try and see the horse's point of view and think only of some far off goal they wish to accomplish—and of course, out of this comes the frustration, anger and chaos that can be seen in our riding. Tom has taught me to slow down and take one step at a time—to try and treat the *disease* and not the symptoms of the problem. Often this is a very basic and simple thing to correct, but has grown into a big problem before I finally realize that something is wrong. Tom has tried to make us all *aware* of what is going on in the horse—the straightness—the attitude and especially what is happening on the *inside* of the horse—how he feels about himself—is he relaxed, confident, happy? Riding with Tom has made me strive for these qualities and not settle for less. It is so easy for me to get lost at times, and lose sight of what I want to accomplish. I often feel that I am going backwards and not progressing at all but usually these are times where I learn the most, realizing that I don't know anything and once again need to listen to the horse—to open up—give up—and be quiet. As Tom so often says—it's the darkest hour before the dawn—the time when the horse and rider come through . . . Another phrase which Tom uses a lot is "prepare to position." I have been trying to help the horse by allowing him the room to prepare himself for what I am asking. I compare this to driving a car. I try not to ask the horse to do anything, the horse is in "neutral," a kind of "emptiness or space," where you feel the horse is waiting for your direction. The horse is attentive and ready to move or do what the rider asks—the rider must also at this time have a clear *picture* of what he or she wants. I have always watched in amazement while Tom rides any horse commanding their complete attention and rewarding them with understanding, love and a clear idea of what they are to do. Tom never seems to lose the connection with the horse that we all only experience briefly.

Most important, Tom has shown us all what the horse has to offer *us* and not the reverse—that riding combines not only the technical aspects, but also the harmony, beauty and spirit of the horse that make us as riders strive for those few moments when horse and rider become one.

—o—

At least for me, it's the consistency. Like Tom was working on me with my horse. The big thing about him was, as Tom described it, *he was sucking his thumb.* My tendency is sometimes I back off too long and let the horse have too much time. Pretty soon they are sitting there loafing around, doing nothing.

What I am trying to do is read the horse accurately so that I am clear about what really needs to be done. Each horse is different and needs to be read clearly so the rider can be effective.

I *think* too much lots of times. If I think too much I can't get in there at the right time and do what intuitively I know to do, because I am being too intellectual about it. You know, like this foot is here, that foot is there, which is all part of it too, but if you take that much time thinking sometimes you don't do it at the right time. The time goes by.

I have a very difficult time when Tom comes sometimes, because Tom is trying to have me think with those feet—and I think, if I don't think about feet I have a better feel.

Tom was saying lift up that time on that foot, and by the time I'm looking at that foot I'm getting the timing all screwed up. Whereas if I just flow with it I don't get it screwed up as much. But there are times to stop and look at the feet and connect the feeling with what you are seeing. So that you *can* do it intuitively.

One day I was telling Tom that I was learning to fly a plane. My point was it's a lot the same no matter what you are doing—and I was trying to force the plane to land. I wasn't allowing the plane to settle down on the ground. I was trying to put it down on the ground but, of course, every time I would make a rough landing. The guy that was teaching me was saying, "Just let the plane land." Telling this to Tom, I saw the little sparkles in his eye and knew I was making my own point, *let* the horse do what you want—don't get in his way.

Later on that day I was backing Jake up and I was finally getting better timing with his feet and Tom said, "It's just like flying the plane." That's very true. We all want to get in our own way and make it happen and we need to just let it happen. But then you have the horse that is a little slow with his feet, and if you don't help him he's not going to do it; as Tom says, "He'll sit there and suck his thumb."

What you see in Tom is a definite confidence. He knows how to set it up and he knows he will succeed. When you portray that attitude to the horse that also helps. But lots of times you get on and you go, "Oh?" Gosh, you're trying real hard but the little voice inside you is saying, "I don't know if this is right or not?" and that gets in your way.

You have to get on there and say, "Yes, maybe I'll make some mistakes and I might miss the timing and maybe I'll screw up worse for a while, but I gotta know I will succeed." You have to always keep that in the back of your mind. It's so easy to get bogged down in your thoughts.

It's real hard to get Tom on a horse, and he's right when he says, "I don't like to get on a horse if I can help you come through yourself." That's very true, but it is a great benefit to see him up on a horse because the more you get to know, of course, the more you know you don't know; but also it trains your eye very well because you can now see what Tom is doing and begin to understand that.

It's real difficult what we do when we ride in an arena because there is no real purpose for the horse—they aren't going after a cow. They aren't doing a job. The main purpose is pleasure for us. So that is why we have such big ego problems in what we do because there is no purpose. It would be much easier if we had to go out and move cattle. Get the job done, keep 'em busy. This way you really get yourself in the way perhaps easier than if the cow were there. I would love to put my mare to work doing cattle.

With her problems you have to get that before they are up that much—a long ways before it happens. That's where our problem is. We get it so far along that we've got a big problem, and it's so hard on the horse to go back and correct that.

I'm trying to read that horse. They are subtle, but they are always telling you what they are going to do. It seems the more I get to know my mare the more I can get to her before she gets to me. She's been tremendous on that for me, because she really will let you have it—if you don't get her first. First she tells me in a whisper and if I don't listen she gives me a hell of a buck and she'll send me flying—usually I step in around the bucks. That's what is great about horses—they are so totally honest.

—o—

I'm still not exactly sure what you want but have finally at last set myself down and started in. Thought maybe I would write down some of the general ideas that come to mind when I think of my experiences with Tom.

One thing I remember Tom saying on my first visit with him, before we started on the horse, was, "I can't teach you anything. I can only help you learn." Probably many people think, like Tom probably suspected I did, that if only they could work with Tom what a great hand they would be. Well, it doesn't take long to figure out that Tom can plant the seed and help along some with the growing, but the real learning has to come from within oneself.

Even I have seen many an over-enthusiastic student cooled off fast when they find it's not a bunch of secret training tips but ways you can work on yourself.

My time with Tom helped me a lot with the horses, but also with cattle, with dogs, with my children and life in general. He got me to thinking about looking at a problem through the eyes of the animal or person you are having it with, to be considerate of how they may be looking at the situation. Many times we are trying so hard to figure a way out of a problem that we overlook the simplest and most obvious solution.

Tom impressed upon me, too, how important it is to get so that you know what you are doing that makes something work in your favor, so that you can apply those principles to something you are trying that doesn't work so well. I've seen cowboys that could drive an old lame, half mad cow up a steep hill and stick her through a real unhandy gate but couldn't load their horse in a horse trailer. When he asked the lame cow to pull the hill, if she just looked the way he wanted her to go he eased off. If she made a few steps that way he rewarded her efforts by letting her rest a little before he asked her to take a few more; but when his horse finally put one foot up in the trailer, that's right when he'd get whacked over the rump.

When I went to work with Tom, the problem that needed the most attention was that I was getting my horses going in a way that was bothering them. Although it seemed to be rare that they would ever buck with me, it was this unsureness and lack of confidence that was causing them to get lost and buck with whoever happened to get them after me.

Tom helped me get a horse going without so much force and tight-ness. It's not that a man doesn't get firm once in a while but these things he helped me with just help your horse learn to get going in a way that helps develop the picture of togetherness that will make you both happier. It's not that I was a mean guy or anything—I just didn't know any better.

I could see that Tom really liked horses, and I think in order to succeed with these methods you really need to. I think you need to have a sympathetic attitude toward horses. A horse has got to be happy and enjoy working for you. I really like to see a horse with a good happy eye. One time I remember going to the fairgrounds here in Elko with a friend to pick up a horse. While waiting for the friend to get his horse, I saw a girl around thirteen or fourteen riding a young horse around the stables. I have never forgotten the look in his eye. He reminded me of, maybe you've seen a fat fuzzy puppy going for a walk with a child. He'll be prancing along out in front of the child and his eyes seem to sparkle and his tongue will be sticking out and he just looks like he's happy to be alive—that's the way this horse looked. The girl was pretty fat and her rig was really old and cracked; but when they went to go somewhere they went together. It was like the girl would say, "Hey ya! Let's go see what's going on over there." I got a chance to strike up a conversation with her, and she said the colt was a mustang, which wasn't hard to believe from his looks, and she made it real plain she really loved him, and he looked like he knew it. Course I know he probably wasn't handy but she wasn't asking him to be handy. She was happy with him the way he was. But, anyway, the look in his eye was what stuck in my mind. I know that is the look I need in my horse's eye. It's just something you don't see too often.

I remember Tom reminding me that if something isn't working out for you like you would like, don't worry about it because you are liable to be trying too hard and trying to force it to happen, and it just doesn't work that way. I remember him saying, "You need to be the horse's master, but him not the slave, but rather your willing partner." You need to learn to wait for things to happen.

Sometimes your horse will know what you want and be trying, but it just takes time for him to coordinate himself for it. Tom gave the example of someone telling you to hit a nail with a hammer in your left hand. You know what the person wants, you try, but you need some time to coordinate yourself. Someone can put the pressure on you to get good at it, but then you have that standing in the way of what you are trying to accomplish. Tom would say that you must be able to determine whether your horse is loafing or just doesn't understand. And most of the time it's not presented by the rider in such a way that the horse can understand it so he gets more pressure put on him to compensate for the rider's lack of understanding and ability; and that's why his eye just won't look like the young girl's horse's eye.

Now sometimes you have to put a horse under pressure to help him become happy. But it's the application and outcome of that pressure that makes the difference. The happiest children I see, also, seem to be the most well disciplined.

Tom worked a lot with me on straightness and evenness. You may have to use quite a lot of firmness to get him straight and even. But if he is not straight and even you are not going around together and he is likely not to be too happy being drug around where it's not 100 percent his idea.

I am really thankful for my time with Tom. I remember him talking of being frustrated that he hadn't really gotten across to anyone what he really had hoped to, and I know I am one more on that list, but I do know that he has made life a lot better for me and a whole bunch of horses.

—o—

I have really enjoyed the time Tom has spent with me and my horses. I have not been able to spend enough time with Tom, but I hope to spend more time in the near future. Tom's advice has helped me with my horses and also with life in general. It is hard to write down all the help and how it works.

For example, if some problem with your horse keeps bothering you and you keep concentrating on correcting that problem, sometimes the harder you work at trying to correct this problem the worse it gets. From Tom I learned to ignore the problem yet still be aware of it. Don't let it keep bothering you and almost always the problem will disappear. He told me to not worry about the big problem, just to break it up into small problems—then to work on each small problem. When I solved each little problem I found I no longer had a *big problem*.

Another thing Tom has made me aware of is to get your horse to travel in a straight line. Even though you may think you are riding in a straight line, one side of your horse might not be moving with the same life as the other side. It has made me aware that both sides should have the same amount of life. It is a pleasure to ride a horse that has the life brought right up through his whole body.

—o—

There are hundreds of things that come to mind that Tom has helped with as I work with different problems (or situations, as Tom calls them). I believe the most vivid things he has instilled in me are to realize where the horse is today, ride him from where he is today, and when it is time to go on the road, to the acceptance of new things.

Being ropers, this has helped my brother and me a great deal. The first time I met and worked with Tom he really helped me on getting green colts accustomed to having a rope swung on them. He made me realize the *fine line* one works on as you deal with this introduction to the horse. This fine line realization has helped me hundreds of times with many different situations. I had a colt that was really afraid of a rope. So Tom just told me to raise my right hand with no rope in it two or three times. After the colt accepted that, I put one coil of my rope in my hand and did the same thing. The colt then got used to that so I took one swing and put another coil in my loop. The horse moved. Tom stopped me, told me to stop swinging if the colt moved, then start the same thing over again. This colt was *really* green and didn't know to move out yet, so I was really accomplishing two things at once. Anyhow, this went on for a while. Finally the colt would stand for one swing, so I went on to two or three. Naturally the colt would move, and here is where the *fine line* thing comes in. Tom told me to swing my rope twice, then stop, and so on. Pretty quick I could feel the colt get ready to move and I would stop swinging so as not to push him over the line, then start over again. It wasn't but a few minutes that I could swing my rope until my arm gave out. This made me realize this fine line tolerance and acceptance barrier that a horse and even a man has.

As I have said before, I use this great tool to help me introduce myself and my thoughts to my horses in hundreds of different situations. Knowing and respecting this makes things so much easier and enjoyable for my horse and me.

—o—

It took me time to start to know, understand and trust Tom. I do all these things now.

I'm just going to jot down, off the top of my head, things I think I understand; they are not necessarily in order of priority.

The horse can't talk but he communicates by body movement or non-movement, by the way he breathes, by the way he smells.

The horse is playful, likes to eat, likes to interact with other horses and animals, and many times likes to do things for a human if given a chance. A generous horse will really put out for his person if the person believes in him, that is, asks him to do something and lets him do it.

Therein lies the difficulty. How do you ask in such a way that the horse understands and *wants* to perform with enthusiasm *your* will which is not necessarily his own? Tom says you need to make it his idea. How do you do that? It seems there are certain times when there is the least resistance to the horse learning something from his rider. One of these times is just after the horse has taken his attention from something away from his rider. If the rider asks just at that moment the horse is most likely to obey. Also when the horse is set on a certain course and the rider asks for another course, and once set on that course the rider asks for another course—this also will start the horse to wondering where his rider would like to go next and thinking of his rider's will.

The communication between horse and rider starts from the moment they make contact (voice, movement, touch). The reality often is that the rider wants the horse to do something that isn't his wish, and he sees no real benefit in doing it. Also a reality is the fact that the horse is much stronger than the rider. So there is a need for domination which can't be domination, but must become a tenuous partnership with mutual respect. And yet I as a rider know that there are certain things I *need* for the horse to do, and that if I can't get those I'm not really riding.

I feel my problem is how to get my horse to want to go, and once he is going I feel that I need him to go in a certain way. I feel that that way is most fulfilling for him, but what a presumptuous statement to make. How can I presume to tell such a magnificent animal how he should move. So I vacillate between trying to skillfully ask (demand) what I want, and trying to listen, look, touch and feel the essence of who he is and his needs. Confusions!

Pain inflicted by me does not seem to be the answer. Discomfort inflicted by the horse to himself is a good teaching tool. Back to Tom and his idea of allowing the horse to be comfortable when he is doing what you want and causing him to be uncomfortable when he is not. (Getting in his way for undesired behavior, and staying out of his way for desired behavior.)

I could go on and on.

—o—

I had trouble with my horse tipping his shoulders and anticipating turns. When we would go to turn, he would fall on his inside shoulder and become very stiff. Tom had me do small circles with lots of changes of direction, especially when one side felt good and he was well balanced. When he was balanced he could change directions smoothly. Going one way he was able to fall on his shoulder easier and it was hard to get him off it. When this happened, I would go straight for a few steps to get him balanced again. Soon he was able to turn both ways smooth and easy.

After we got that down, my horse started sticking his outside shoulder out. Our turns were fairly easy, but he didn't move forward with a lot of energy, just barely enough, and I had to work to keep him going. Tom had me tickle him on the outside shoulder with a stick and he would straighten up. Then he had me practice turns from a standstill. When we would go to turn, my horse would start to reach with his outside shoulder and spin around his inside shoulder. He should have been starting with his inside front so he could stay balanced and have his hind end work better under him. I had to set my horse's feet up by backing up his inside front a stride, then I asked him to turn and he had to strike off with his inside front. Then later I would just turn his head one way and his front inside foot would start off automatically and his hind end would be working well, too.

In backing up, my horse would sometimes drift off one way or another instead of backing up straight. When I was backing, one side wasn't taking as long a stride back as the other, so he couldn't go straight. Tom had me feel his feet moving and fill in on the rein a little longer on the side that dragged. He had me fill in more so his hind foot would take a longer stride back too. Pretty soon he began to back a lot straighter and easier.

Tom also had me practice being able to choose which foot I wanted him to start off with, going back and forward. My horse tended to start and stop usually with one particular side. I worked at keeping a soft feel on the reins and asking for a particular foot and pretty soon I had his feet right in my hands and we could do anything.

I also had trouble with my halts. When we went to stop, he wasn't able to keep himself together. He would just slur into it and get heavy in front. This carried over to all his other gaits; when I went to ask more of him and to ask him to collect himself, he couldn't. He would be still in front and his hind end couldn't come under him. He was okay on a long rein; his feet would move pretty well but when I'd ask more of him it wasn't very easy for him and his tail would start to get busy. This was all from his taking a hold in front instead of keeping his hind end coming and his front end free.

I practiced a few transitions, keeping my legs on him and taking a feel of the reins and asking him for a transition. When he started to get hard in front, I would keep my legs on him and keep asking; sometimes he would need a little nip on the rein to get soft. When he was soft, I was soft, but not throwing him away.

I practiced keeping him soft and being able to move him out, and bring him back and stay light. When he was light, moving easy and staying together, he was right there and we could do anything. Soon he was automatically there when I asked, and it is getting easier for him to stay there all the time, nice and soft.

—o—

You have to know what you are setting up and then you have to know how long you wait. Do you wait five minutes—depending on what horse you are working with. If you are working with a horse that is not real willing to be with you—how long do you wait? I know each day is a little different because the horse feels different every day. My temperament isn't always the same even though I'm trying to work on keeping it the same, so the horse knows that I'm going to be the same all the time. But, I'll work with a horse that maybe is independent and really doesn't feel he needs people too much. That is where I have a problem. Do I have to come on stronger with him at times, or back off, because I have had him feeling like velvet. It's a feeling that there's velvet in my hands, and there is velvet. All I do is think things and they happen. I almost don't have to set him up even though I'm thinking of setting him up, but I'm not really doing anything because he is just so *there* for me.

Then there are days when he is not there for me. How do I get him there? This is what I am going through. What did I do the day before to get him there?

To me, the experimentation of hands and legs—the combination of hands and legs, the balance between the hands and legs—is very important for my horse. I think this is what Tom is trying to point out when he comes over to us. Each horse is different and it's all going to take different time and different pressure with each horse, because you are literally dealing with the horses' minds and they are all just so different. Everyone else is different too. Sometimes some riders just don't get along with that horse's mind, with that horse.

It's helped me so much not just for working forward but the other things, for extensions in the trot, for canter work, for the lateral work. It all has to be the same feeling, not just to go forward with this lightness; that isn't enough; you have it in every single movement that you're asking from the horse. That's what Tom was trying to get through to me, and I have picked it up. I really have.

What I got, also, from Tom last time is—I was sitting on my horse's hind feet, the front end was up and all I had to do was just sit there; just be careful not to mess that part up because the horse had given that to me. But I didn't know how I'd gotten it even though I knew the feel was right. "I had him light as a feather and doing everything." I felt that I almost didn't have to be there. I didn't need the reins. I could just sit down and he would turn around on his hind feet without any effort as long as I didn't get in his way. When I find I do get in his way—that helps me *not* get in his way.

When I have that problem is when the feet feel like they are up into their knees and you are waiting and you are waiting and you are waiting, and there's nothing happening and you almost feel like you are sitting on the front end instead of the hind end. But I think I'm getting it sorted out a little bit.

A lot of people I have seen and heard talking about their horses don't have anything nice to say about their horses. The horse is always "out to get them"—and the horse picks up on that. It is like a picture in your mind. Whatever picture I have is what comes through, and I might have the wrong picture; sometimes I think I do. But a lot of the time I have the right picture and that picture will come through, whereas a lot of people have a picture that the horse is out to get them. The horse won't do this and the horse won't do that. I try to tell them, "Are you making it possible for the horse to do that?" "Have you got too much bend somewhere—or too much angle somewhere so the horse can't do it?" But they do—I've seen them and they do.

So, it's this attitude thing that I think Tom is real terrific on—at least I've picked that up from Tom. Watching him on Jake the other day was something I'll never forget, ever—ever—ever.

Have you ever had a day, though, when you don't want to get on? I have days when I do not want to get on. Then I've had days, like today, when I can't wait to get on because I think I came through something yesterday. I was the one that sweated yesterday and I think I came through something and I can't wait to get back on today, to see if what I found along with my horse will work again today or whether it is just something that was a fluke.

One thing that I have a hard time with is, I have this feeling that most horses would rather not work if they were given the choice. With my horse's temperament, he can get real stuck in the ground with his feet. He is kind and steady, and I feel he would rather just take care of the barn all day and make sure the horses are in their right stalls and tell them what to eat and tell me what time to feed—just keep a check on the whole area.

I really think in the long run if I can get that working for me, I'm going to have a wonderful horse. But what I'm trying to say and I don't know how to say this, is with a horse, if you set it up right, you are in good shape, but if you miss somewhere and you don't set it up right, I find this horse will get out of hand.

Sometimes I'm too hard on myself. At times I think, "God, I'm causing all these problems and I know this horse can do it because I've already done it on him, say a week ago." If I get too hard on myself that's when my confidence gets real shattered and I find myself getting off him quite a bit and walking around thinking, "All right, what feel am I missing?" Or, "What is he missing, too?" It works both ways; I got into a place where I started blaming myself 90 percent of the time. That's not going to help him.

Then I had to come on a little bit stronger to make sure my horse understood I wasn't this little pansy thing, without any confidence.

So, I think you've got to stop and think, OK now, what kind of horse is this; you need to get into his personality and then you go from there. I think you need to have a real clear path toward what you want.

Something I bumped into and I finally admitted to myself is that when I feel the horse and everything is there, it is real easy to feel it; but there's another place when the horse is real irked about something and he is real hard in all the corners, and in the poll, in the mouth, and everywhere. Then it is real hard for me to feel that place opening up, real hard for me to point it out to the horse. He gets so he feels like a building—like the Empire State Building—and I can't quite find the soft place. I can't point out to him where the soft place is and block all the other places.

I don't think I'm trying to make it happen. I am trying to point it out to him more than to make it happen.

That is what I found out yesterday: that I've gotta be at that point right before it happens.

Some people won't be there for the whisper. I have not been there for the whisper. I've been there when it's gotten so, "Oh, I need to be there!" and that is what was pointed out to me the other day. Yesterday, all day, all I thought about is not that inch—not that inch—you can't get that inch ahead of me to where it is going to be ten feet, and then I have to step in and I have a terrible time. That's what Tom says is "listening to the horse," but sometimes I listen too late.

It's really dawned on me the last couple of days what we are talking about right now, whereas before I'd feel something going on and maybe it was leading up to this bad place but I didn't know what to do about it. So sometimes you have to reach that bad place before you know to go back.

I think when Tom was first coming I didn't understand what he was talking about, not one thing. Then with the help of my friends, I think we probably hashed thousands of hours of this over, among all of us. Then all of us have different feels—and all of us have different ways of thinking. It was kind of tricky for me to pick up my own feel—my own way of thinking—because I would love to be like Tom and I know I never will be, but if I could be a little bit like him my own life would be much softer.

I'm finally, after three years, starting to understand what Tom is trying to tell us all. It's taken that long for me. Maybe I'm not too smart, but it's taken me a whole long time. I think part of my problem was fear, the fear of having this big horse do something and injure me.

I'm not fearful of the big powerful movements, but I was fearful. In other words, I really didn't know the horse well enough to stop and feel—and I feel that's real important.

I think it is all feel, and how do you teach feel? How do you teach experience? I was used to someone telling me what to do. Now I run into so many, many things I forget—maybe a lot of us do—to look back, three years back, and remember where the horse was and where he is now—look at this, at the progress he has made. I mean it is tremendous progress, and I forget to look back. I maybe look back to last week, but look back three years ago, where your horse was then and where he is now. He is tremendous, and I forget to compliment my horse for that.

Thanks to Tom, I work on the whole horse: the corners of the horse, the neck, the head—almost every muscle of the horse so they are soft— the softness and relaxation plus the movement, the big tremendous stride. Tom is the one who has shown me this; maybe I just have a little bit.

I do know, with Tom's method, if you can get it, just a little bit, it will last forever. It will always be there. No matter if that horse has a year off and you're the same, it will be there—the horse will have it and there's always more. This is what Tom has shown us: there is more there—if we would just give the horse a chance.

—o—

In reference to our conversation about feedback to the past association with Tom in previous clinics—I am outstandingly impressed with the in-depth perception that Tom has, not only with the horse but also with the individual he is working with. Also, he misses nothing that is going on around him.

I have sat and studied him while he is studying other people and horses, and probably me at the same time. He may be talking to someone directly in front of him, but if someone off to the left or right, or even behind him, is having difficulty with his horse, Tom knows it and sees it immediately. He reminds me of the real sharp, wide-awake colt that sees every movement that is going on and doesn't miss a thing.

There are two instances that come to my mind. One is the work Tom did with me on the sorrel mare that I was riding, which was basically going back to his idea of making the good thing easy and the bad thing difficult.

The good thing was to move out and travel off in a free and easy manner with ears up and looking where she was going. The bad thing was that she was wanting to hang up and stay with the other horses, and when she did leave it was with protest.

Tom has the in-depth perception to see that all that was necessary was a slight amount of more effort on my part to *prepare* her before asking her to move off.

The next case that comes to mind is the work that he did with the girl on her black mare with whom she was having trouble changing leads. Tom's suggestion was that the rider should try to emphasize to lift the feet higher off the ground. My first thought was, how in hell do you lift the feet any higher than the horse is lifting them? It was something that I hadn't even noticed. The mare was not lifting her feet very high off the ground, which interfered with her lead change. But Tom's keen eye and perception had noticed this right off. Not only was he able to diagnose the cause, he also had a prescription for a cure.

—o—

I have thought a lot about the feedback you asked for. I am not sure I even know what you want. I think you want to know how I feel Tom has helped me, and where I am today with the horse. I find that hard to answer. I have had help from Tom, Ray and Bill, and I think they have all tried to tell me some of the same things, some of which have sunk in. But it is hard for me to decipher just where it has all come from.

I know that what took place at the Bozeman clinic two years ago meant quite a bit to me. Tom tried to impress upon us the importance of getting our horses to line out and stay straight. Then at the Elko clinic that same year, he had us riding around without using our reins. I felt something there that really stayed with me. Since then I have been able to keep my horses with me a little better. I am not sure just what is taking place, but it helps me with all my colts. I think I am still missing something and keep thinking I am going to get a break-through, but I don't quite get there.

I am not sure just where I am with my horses or if I could even describe it if I did know. It seems like I change my thinking every day.

—o—

I rode a four-year-old colt I had broke at home in Tom's clinic, here with Ray. I remember mostly how kind Tom was. He took plenty of time with everyone and hurried neither horses nor people. He was a confidence builder for me. My colt had never developed a lope—he was stiff and insisted on galloping. Tom had me gallop, and trot into that—the colt was not supple enough to go from the walk departs and not collected enough to lope; if he got too slow he disunited. We did not work on head position until the colt was balanced. So we did a lot of anxiety-free galloping (not really fast, but not at a slow pace, either) in lots of large circles.

I watched Tom diagnose and cure a tail wringing mare at that clinic. Her rider was instructed where to sit in his saddle—he had been too far back and it annoyed the mare. When the rider's position was corrected, the mare's rigid back relaxed and she quit wringing her tail, which had nothing to do with spurs or leg aids.

He also explained to a boy whose colt would unaccountably bog his head and go to bucking how to anticipate it and why the colt did it. The colt would be jogging along quiet but suddenly he would become unsure of his rider or anything else, and this panicked him. So he'd just go to bucking. To cure it, Tom showed the rider how to watch the colt's ears and inside eye and when the *first* sign of insecurity showed up, the rider was to give the colt a "job" that he understood how to do, like make a circle or change speed. It worked—the colt quit blowing up.

I was riding a two-year-old stallion at home and found that the colt, though kind, would seem to forget that I was around and begin to act as if he were playing in the pasture which included running and crow hopping while we were just riding down the road.

Disconcerting! I called Tom on the phone and told him that it seemed that the colt would just forget I was there but that I didn't want to keep "bugging" him for no reason if he was trotting along quietly.

Tom explained a little of the nature of a stallion to me. He said that they notice more things than other horses and are always looking around and observing. He said I needed to keep the colt occupied. Instead of riding down the road putting on miles as I thought I was doing, I should give him specific little chores like making "snake" trails among the sagebrush. Get off the road and ride little winding turns, keeping the colt's mind busy with the rein and leg aids needed to make lots of snake trails. Also to make walk-to-trot-to-walk transitions and to make trot-to-lope-to-trot-to-walk-to-stop transitions and to let him stand for a moment, holding the rein still until he took a step back and then go do something else. I was to find stuff to walk over and cows to follow, and I did all of these things and they worked like a charm. I built a little simple trail course with logs and bridges and tires, and tarps and barrels to back through. It's just like teaching a smart kid; a person must give him enough things to do that are hard, to keep him interested without giving him too much and frustrating him.

—o—

The biggest thing is just thinking about this thing and keeping your mind straight. Like getting the horse to perform for you and him wanting to do it. Not keeping him confused—or upsetting the horse to do something.

This is the stage I'm in right now. In the past whenever I had a problem with a horse—like a lead change or a spin or stop or something like that—I didn't worry about keeping the horse from getting excited about it and upset.

In the past, you know, you never worried about upsetting the horse. You just went ahead and did it. You said, "Whoa," and that was it. It was "whoa" right *there*. The thing that I think about Tom, that he's done most for us, is to get this horse to perform or do a maneuver, or something, we now try to keep him from getting upset. He tells us to do it without upsetting the horse. It's one of the greatest things. But this whole thing is a way of life. It doesn't have to do with horses particularly—that is the reason it is so great. For me, it's changed my whole attitude on life.

My whole philosophy is—if you don't live it you don't believe it. Now this is real hard to perform all the time—I'm just like everybody else—I'm sure you don't always perform. You have expectations and perfection that you are striving for, but you don't get there. It is a hard thing to do. It's the same with the horses. It's pretty easy to be asking for a soft feel and trying to get these horses to perform for you so they aren't bothered; and *then* reach a point in there where you are flustered and the horse is flustered and you revert back. Occasionally you'll go out there and run into the fence for a while, or something like that.

I think this is one of the things Tom tries to explain—to think this thing out.

Tom has done some marvelous things that I have seen at these clinics, and you stand around and say, "My God! How does he get it to happen?" But Tom, he believes this so he lives it. He lives this thing, see—and I think you have to become more and more aware of these things and live it—as well as think it.

But a lot of times the thought is one thing, the execution is something else. It's like we used to talk in those clinics. They'd say, "Do you have a question?" Well, if you knew enough to ask the question you could pretty well answer usually, if you'd stop and think—but it's whether you can execute it or not. This is the thing I run into a lot of times, and I feel very inadequate to communicate with the horse.

I ride every day—I ride all day—this is what I do for a living, but I feel very inadequate in staying out of the way of this horse, at times. You're wanting him to go left and he is thinking right—so you are in his way.

The people who are really dedicated to this and wanting it real bad, it has changed their way of thinking—to think about the horse instead of *making* him do their thing. It's not easy.

Especially a person, like myself, that has been really rough on these horses. Hell! Nobody could beat, or spin and slash, any better than I could. I had had lessons from experts on this, you know—and I could pound and beat with the best of them. In the past, before I got to working with Tom and Ray at these clinics, about all my horses ever learned in life was to get out of my way. They would be at a place and if I wanted to go *there* or stop *here*, the horse had to *get*, and get out of my way. Well, now I am starting to think about letting those things happen. When you are in time it all happens real smooth, but if you are a little bit late, or a little bit early, then you run into these problems again. But these problems come up less often—and I guess this is a tribute to Tom and Ray—that if I stop and think about it I can make it right or make some progress. This is the thing you do and it's a way of life. It is a way of thinking.

Lots of people are looking for a mechanical part of the horse. They make all sorts of gimmicks and devices for that. I don't worry so much about that now as keeping my mind in the right frame—to always be aware of these things. You have to get aware of everything about those horses—their feet and their mind and their position. That is one of the biggest problems: when things happen people cease to become aware. Consequently, one of the greatest things we've learned from these clinics is to be more aware and to start thinking more—using your own mind.

Boy! I see it every day. I could load a bull elephant in a trailer if I am by myself; but you get some people here, and they are going to help you, you know. Well—the best thing they can do is to go over there and sit down in the shade of the barn—'cause I don't need any help—I don't want it—'cause when the horse starts he is going to force it through—but it's such a mental thing with horses. And I can't even scratch the surface on this thing—my inadequacies of not being able to do this or comprehend these things.

Everybody was sitting around there in Elko that year when they watched Tom ride this black horse. This little teenage girl was riding him. He was running off with her—a total disaster. So what happens is Tom asked her if he could ride her horse; and she seemed tickled to death to let him ride. Tom gets on and in a few minutes Tom has the reins lying over the saddle horn and his arms folded and he is jogging the horse in circles and loping the horse in circles. Before this, that little girl was just hanging on, trying to keep him from running off with her. Well! It's his mental thing with these horses.

I was having some trouble with a lead change on this sorrel horse. He was a real left handed horse when I got him, which it seems most horses are. So, I concentrated a lot on the right side, working, trying to soften the right side up and getting the life in there. Then you do what usually happens; you get the horse in and he is more right handed than he is left handed. So the lead changes were a problem for him. He was a horse that had been ridden before and kind of had some "people problems" there.

He would start to make the change, and he would charge the change, want to run through it. Well, I'm starting to finally get far enough along that I can see the trueness in a horse and keep him true and keep him up straight when he is cantering or loping, and the softness in there. I wanted my lead changes to be just like the other part of my circle. All the way around the circle he was up straight. I wanted a smooth lead change. You could come to this lead change and you could just feel him swell. He's a horse that is pretty hot anyway. He'd just swell up and it would scare him, see. I was scaring him on the lead changes, and the same thing on the stop. He'd swell and get scared. I talked to Charlie on the phone about it, and he was telling me about picking the inside rein, raising your hand on the inside and tipping that nose and then arcing the body. Well, often the horse that's missing that lead, his body is concaved the wrong way to make the lead change. Then I went back and listened to tapes of past clinics. I got back to trying to get out of his way and let him do it, and now it's smoothed up right.

I think the horse will teach you, as much as anything, if we can tune ourselves to being observant of this. I think that's the way Tom learned. I don't know Tom's history that way or anything—but to me I'm sure Tom had the time and the patience and the foresight to study the horse, and he says the horse taught him what he knows. He gives the horse the credit. So basically if we were all sharp enough—if we were all as intelligent as Tom and as smart as he is about this thing— we'd all just sit back and let the horse teach himself.

The greatest thing in the world about this is the self-satisfaction. There has to be a certain amount of self-satisfaction riding these horses. If you don't get a self-satisfaction out of what you are achieving, then you had better quit, because there are going to be days that you can't show a lot of progress as far as visible things; but it's a mental thing.

I had a horse here and I had him in the bridle. He was a darn good little horse. I had roped on him, a lot of stuff like this. A friend of mine came down and got on him. This little horse wasn't a trained horse or a broken horse, but he was a horse that was pretty advanced. My friend rode him a bit, and he stopped him a couple of times, then he said, "I never rode a horse that had the balance in his stop like that." He said, "He sure does stop." I said, "He's kind of a natural—he just does it 'cause he wants to." He said, "Yeah! But he knows he God-damned sure better want to!"

I got to thinking about it. This guy knew me from the past. That's about the way it would have been in the past before Tom and Ray.

I never will forget when I went to that first clinic down in Orena. I came home here and I had a colt tied up down there at the hitching rack. I was saddling him up, or doing something with him, and he flew back. Well, I just bristled. That son-of-a-gun wasn't going to do that. I grabbed the cheek of the halter and went to kicking him in the belly— and I kicked and kicked and I was give-out. The colt was standing there huffing and puffing and all worked up, and I was leaning on him catching my breath and I got to thinking.

"Boy, you are one smart son-of-a-gun. You go down there and spend eighty-five dollars (eighty-five dollars to me at that time was a lotta money). You go down there and you give a guy eighty-five bucks to teach you something different and show you a better way and you come home and you go right back to doing the same thing you've always done."

I got to thinking that was really smart. Here I blow eighty-five bucks I didn't have, then revert right back. Ever since that—from that day on—I've tried to improve. For this part of the country this thing has been a great influence.

I know when I came back from that first clinic, I didn't know Tom, but I had heard Ray mention him. I came back and I was telling a friend about roping the horse by the hind foot, and he said, "That sounds like what Tom Dorrance used to do." Then I said, "Yeah, that's the fellow who taught this guy. Tom's the one that's worked with him."

It's funny how my attitude has changed. Years ago we used to trail the cows up and down here all over the country—and invariably you're going to have one break out—and break down over the side of the bank, or go into some field if the gate's open, or something like this. Well, boy, I used to get after them. I'd run up there and I'd cuss and run them back on the road. Well, any more if that old cow goes it's probably my fault for not being on the ball to get there in time and being ahead of her, but those things don't upset me anymore. I say we'll just jog around this one and put her back over here. Something like that, and it's the same way with the horses. I never get mad at them anymore. It has tempered me. You never have to work on the horse, because the horse is always right. You hear Tom say that all the time.

The horse is right, you know—but you do have to say what's the problem here—I don't understand you and you don't understand me.

Another thing that I have put a lot of faith in is that the horse will do anything that I want him to do and probably any way that I want him to, if he understands what I want him to do. Used to be when I would work with a horse, I was going to teach him to stop, or teach him to spin, or teach him to back up. This train of thought changes that completely around, because I know the horse can already spin faster than I can ride—and he can stop and he can go, smooth and true. All you do is get the mind so you can communicate with it. Tom has found the road to communicate. It is a mental thing of finding the way to communicate, because the horse will do anything that you want if he understands what you want. He is living in his complete world.

—o—

This is my observation, but it seems a lot of times right before the horse is ready to come through there is a lot of confusion and a lot of stress going on. You think you are just about ready to lose him, but, in fact, you are just about ready to get him. I think that is a real critical time. If there's any time that I'd say you really need to be there for a horse, it's right before he is ready to break through, because there is a lot of struggling going on. I think his instincts are really operating on a fine tuned sort of system—and if you are not right there for him when he is really, really searching, you could lose him.

I think that is one of the things that Tom really impressed me with, that I am working on. It's a dual sort of thing: it's attitude: my attitude and getting the mind. Those two things were concepts that were really difficult for me to get, because it seems unusual in horsemanship to put the emphasis on getting the horse's mind. It seems an unusual approach. I didn't know for sure what he was talking about when Tom would say, "Is the horse hooking on to you?" "Do you have him?" "Is he there for you?" I kind of knew—but I didn't know, and that is where I am really spending a lot of time—feeling that and working on that. Then, also, I am examining my attitudes. "Why am I doing this? What am I here for? What's my purpose with this horse? How much of my ego is involved? How much of pleasure is involved?"

I think that is something that indirectly Tom emphasizes. He may not use the word attitude or he may not even directly say it, but after you work with him for a while, pretty soon you start thinking, "What am I doing here? What's my function? What's my purpose?" When you start thinking about the mind of the horse—then the two of you connecting—and are you connected and how well are you connected, it changes your whole approach to horsemanship.

When you work with Tom you hear a whole lot about respect and response; and then you have to think about it. What is respect? How much response? One of the things I've learned is to watch the confidence. You really have to know that what you are doing is right, and you need to know that that horse is going to come through for you every time. You've got to have that confidence. You are learning to recognize just the smallest effort coming through for you—and to be able to know when the horse is working at it—and when he is starting to come through for you. If you don't see that and if you don't know to see that—you just have to be around it to know to look for it—an ear— a relaxation in one muscle.

It is a whole different level of awareness and consciousness, or whatever word you want to use, once you start to get into it. It's exciting. It's difficult. It's sometimes even painful. But to me it doesn't ever lose the excitement. Learning in this way is a real exciting thing. Like I wonder what's going to go on today. You are kind of working on something and it's like Tom will say, "Now let the horse soak on it for a while!" and it's kind of exciting to go back the next day and see how much did he soak on it or how much didn't he.

Sometimes when you think you are offering a feel, it doesn't come through to the horse. The other night we were working with my baby colt in our front yard, and I was saying, kind of gingerly, "Come along, little guy; come along, little guy." Even the way I was holding my fingers was gingerly; when you start doing it you're not even aware of it. The fellows were just kind of standing off to one side. Then Joe asked if I needed some help, and I said, "Sure!" He really took ahold of that little guy and received unlimited trust from him, and I could see it, and he kind of pointed it out to me in a real tactful way—made me aware.

He worked with that colt for a while, and he said, "Now this little guy will go just about anywhere you want him to—he is that hooked on now." We were kind of joking around there, and he took the colt right in the front door of the house into the front room, turned him around and brought him back. We were cracking up. He took him into the horse trailer, turned him around and brought him back—and when you see that! Here I was working with the horse first and I thought I had him really hooked on to me, and I wasn't even near.

But a good horseman gets the most he possibly can out of each horse, with the right attitude. In other words, it's almost a sin, in a way, just to get part. Given the right circumstances and the right situation, get the most you possibly can. It's an honor to the horse.

It isn't easy. When one gets tight you just follow along and get tight; that is something I am really, really working on. And maybe sometimes, we are listening the wrong way. In other words, we really are tuned in to when they are coming through for us. Watching the eye— watching the ear—but are we tuned when they are going out? You know when we are losing them. I think it's there before you know it.

You'll hear people say, "I was going along and everything was OK, but all of a sudden I got bucked off." But the horse did tell them. They just didn't know how to read the horse. I think that we emphasize so much having them come to us, but what we have to learn to read is when they are dropping out, too.

I'm sure Tom is going through a lot now in trying to teach this. I had to stop and think how would I explain any of this to someone else.

What fascinates me—he'll say, "Let them work at it, let them work at it." It might be frustrating to you or someone like myself who needs more words to have things explained. But with horses—they don't need the words, so he can set it up for the horse in this non-verbal way, and the horse can learn to come through for him when he lets the horse work at it. He is kind of approaching us from the same way. He gives us as much as he can but it is a little, you know, and we gotta really work at it." It might be frustrating to you or someone like myself who needs work at it.

"Is this it? Is that it?" No. You quit—and then you go on. It's exciting.

—o—

The main thing I've gotten from Tom is there is no way you can force a horse to do anything. No way at all. This I've learned from Tom, and I've learned from my colts. The minute you start forcing is the minute their brain shuts down. And it has to be done in slow—slow—slow steps. Tom has been saying that for five years, and we never believed him. It never sank in or it never registered. The reason it works by going slowly is because they actually learn it, and from that it's praise. *If they don't know they've done right, then they know nothing.* If you don't tell them that they have done right in some way—either by your perfect timing when you ease off, or a pat or reward of some kind, they never look for that. I have just realized how important it is. That's how I have ruined two horses.

—o—

It is not often that one has the opportunity to associate with someone who has become a legend in his own lifetime. I had heard much about Tom Dorrance, mostly from Ray Hunt, and hungered for more, like a drowning man hungering for air.

Finally that opportunity came, and I had the chance to be closely associated with Tom on another project for the last five years. Tom is a great individual with many talents, a great student with profound wisdom, lots of good common sense; but the one thing I admire more than anything else is the self-discipline he has developed. I know of no one whose wants and needs are as close together as Tom's! I have enjoyed many of Tom's abilities, but most of all I have enjoyed his help with the horses and his keen insight into what the horses' viewpoint of the situation would be.

Sometimes Tom is hard to understand, and the things he told me or the answers to my questions wouldn't be clear to me for a long time. Maybe months or even years later, I would get the picture and realize the point he was making. I, like many others, wanted an answer on what you do to get a horse to stop, change leads, spin, etc. I remember one time asking Tom, "How much pressure do you exert on the reins to keep a horse collected but still not get hard?" His answer was typical: "*It all depends.*"

Tom loves a challenge. I remember buying a little paint mare who was really sour. She hated people, other horses, dogs and even herself. She didn't want anyone to touch her, and it seemed like her ears were glued back permanently. When you went to ride her she would switch her tail fast enough to keep all insects at least a hundred feet away. Tom took her on as a special project, and now she likes everybody, comes up to be scratched and likes to cuddle at every opportunity.

I could go on and on, but it's not my talent or place to write a book. I do know, however, that Tom Dorrance is the greatest horseman I have known, and the things he can do with a horse start with very basic thoughts and actions. There are no short cuts or gimmicks used, just timing, feel and balance; no hurry-up methods, just good common sense. Be a student. I really feel it is a privilege to be associated with this man.

—o—

You know Tom is a superb cowman. He was a cowman before he was a horseman. His father had one of the best purebred herds in the northwest. Then, as I understand it, Tom really got into this work with the horses from breaking their work horses. What Tom did for me was, he probably made me a better individual from understanding horses. Because I was a person with a bad temper. I still am, but I can think now, and this was the big thing he got me to doing—thinking that a horse is a living creature with a mind, and trying to understand him.

At the time Tom came I had gotten to the point where I was just going to stick a grazer bit on the horse and do my cowboying, and that was it. I had just gotten to the point where I was so disgusted with myself for fighting horses that I had just quit. Oh, I was going to do my work. Anyway, this is what he did, turned us around to help us understand the horse, and understand people, just turning my whole life around; and I think my brother feels the same way. I know we have talked a lot of times of his making us aware of every living creature.

My boys—Joe won the world saddle bronc championship on account of Tom Dorrance, and Mike was successful at rodeoing. These boys did well, because he turned us around to be a family—a family unit. Everything we got into we were really involved in, and I know that's what made it. Up to the time Tom came it wasn't like that.

I think the other big thing he taught me to do is to *see* what I look at. You know—in everything—horses, cattle, people—to observe and compare.

Tom would say if you are happy the way you are, and you are getting the job done, there is no reason to change—but if you aren't happy then you have to start changing your attitude; and I think this was right. I have seen him be around a lot of guys and not all of them accepted what he had to say. He was frank with them all and left it that way, because they were happy the way they were. The ones that weren't happy with themselves, like myself, went Tom's way because he was showing us a new way, and we're still hunting and working. This gets right back to the people. It is attitude he gets into a person.

A person could go on all night about him, the great things he's done, and most of them you've heard already, from other people. But the things that have really done wonders for me and my horse are things that he told me twenty years ago, that I didn't understand. Every day I'm learning those things now and I am understanding them. But he planted it there all those years ago; at the time I didn't even know what he was talking about; but now as I am getting nearer and nearer they make sense. Each pattern kinda fits in but you always remember back what he told you and at the time it went over my head. He just left it there and didn't push it, and now it is making sense.

There are just times when you gotta work on your own. You need the help—then you gotta work it out. He would always come to us, then he would pack up and go back to Joseph; or go down to see Bill or Ray or somebody—then he'd come back up again. One thing about him, though—if he started something he never left you. You'd think he'd deserted you, but he'd always get back to you. It's funny how he can remember the problems you were having a year before, or two years before. He'd get it worked around to where you'd start in all over. He remembers every minute detail. This, of course, is what makes him so great: his memory. I think you can't be a great horseman, or a great stockman, without a good memory. This is what Tom has—I know I might not see him for a year or two or three, and he just starts right off and that's a great thing; but we don't get enough time to spend with him anymore.

Tom has taught me to learn from each individual, and this is what makes it so exciting.

—o—

These notes are in the rough and not totally complete, but I wanted you to get something.

1. Horse must learn to position to perform on his own—if not, the rider cannot possibly position the horse himself and not be in his way.

2. Horse must be taught to position for movement of any kind. Once he learns to position for a movement the movement becomes easy.

3. There is a time to go very slowly—if you go slowly at this time, you are actually going faster.

4. He must be totally loose in order to move properly—all four corners must be free.

5. If he does not start off from the first step properly (balanced from behind, soft in the front), no sense going at all.

6. Any problems that are present from halt to walk or back to walk will be present in all three gaits.

Tom helped me to feel free to experiment. I learned the importance of getting the horse with me because he wants to be. Everything I do with a horse on the ground carries over to under saddle. Any time I find that I have to use an undue amount of force or pressure my horse gets too upset. I know that I am missing somewhere, not that the horse is misbehaving.

I feel that I am now riding the feet of the horse more and more instead of the body. I am beginning to be able to influence the feet, thereby helping my horse out.

I think about being there to direct when he needs direction. I try to get out of his way when he doesn't.

I can see my horse getting more confidence as he is able to have more control over his movement. I try to get to the feet in my corrections, especially with a problem of tightness or balance.

I am becoming more aware of being in time with my horse, and his feet being in time with each other.

It has changed my whole attitude—opened up a new world. I'm learning to wait for things to happen instead of forcing—just try to set up right.

Getting the horse to come when I reach—to be friendly and enjoy my touch, but not push—to give to pressure anywhere. It's pretty hard to work the energy that he gives me in a constructive way instead of repressing it.

Another thing is not forcing a young horse to move under saddle but helping him to feel that he can move each foot and putting him in a position that he wants to move.

I now notice and look for the soft look in the eye, a relieved sigh, softening of the muscles, especially in the neck.

If the horse or I am uncomfortable, I am missing somewhere.

—o—

Working with Tom is an experience that is almost beyond words. For so many years I had heard about Tom and heard his words quoted and had tried to understand his ways with horses. I never even entertained a thought that some day I might be so fortunate as to work with him. That day did come, however, and it was an experience that helped my thinking in more than horsemanship alone. Tom seems to relate everything in the world in the same way he relates to horses. Just as a horse becomes supple and ready to learn when it is with him, I found myself at ease and in a learning frame of mind almost immediately because of Tom's manners. Since then I've noticed how many of his observations about the horse and how he learns are true of many people and things.

Tom had seen me work with my colt in one of Ray's clinics and I had visited with him on other occasions about various horse problems. A couple of weeks after the clinic I spoke with Tom and he said things looked like they were going pretty well but asked how I liked his trot. I said it was terribly rough and I had a hard time staying with it, as Tom had no doubt noticed. Tom said he thought there were a few things we might try that would help to make the gait more comfortable, if I'd like to try. (If I'd like to try?!!) We agreed he would come over in a few days. Of course, while I waited for the time to come I had to get out and work on the trot myself. I went out in the middle of a big ranch and spent a good long time making this colt trot, trying to extend or collect him or do something to improve the feeling. All I got was a tired colt and a back and neck that felt nearly broken from the jolting! When I called

Tom to see when he could come over, he said, "Well, it's good that you tried some things on your own." I guess he knew then I'd be ready to try something different.

The interesting thing was that when we worked Tom said almost nothing about the trot. He did suggest that I might be more comfortable with shorter stirrups, so we fixed them first. Then, as I struggled to haul myself up onto this tall three-year-old, Tom suggested that both the colt and I would be more comfortable if I found something to stand on while mounting. As I look back, I realize that both of these suggestions represent one of the keys to what Tom does with a horse. Every attention is given to making the animal comfortable, from adjusting the stirrups to finding a way to mount without pulling the animal off balance. When the animal is comfortable, he is better able to do what the rider wants in a way that is also comfortable for the rider.

From this point we worked just on freeing the colt's movements. I told Tom that this colt could move so fast when it was his idea that he would almost get out from under me. However, very often when I'd ask him to move there was little or no response, or on other occasions when I really got after him he might crow hop first and then move out. Tom noted, "So you go to leave before he does." That was exactly it: my body was trying to reach forward and my legs were livening up, but the horse's feet were glued to the ground. Tom showed me some better ways to use my legs—like holding my spurs into the colt's sides and even digging in a little until there was a response, rather than just pounding on him with my legs and feet. As Tom put it, "Don't try to leave without him. Just see if you can wait there until he prepares to leave." Soon the slightest touch of my spurs or even just the pressure of my legs brought up the respect and a response, and we were leaving together.

We also worked on getting the colt to prepare to back by "picking up his feet" with the reins, first one side and then the other, until the colt was backing freely, straight and balanced and without getting stuck anywhere.

That day we were working out in my three-acre pasture, and the colt kept wanting to stay at the low end near the other horses. If I tried to move him out to the far end of the field, he would manage to pull pretty hard to the right, and we'd end up in some manner of a circle. Tom let me work at this problem for a while, but we weren't getting anywhere and pretty soon he asked me to come over and visit with him. He suggested that it seemed like the colt just didn't know he could go to the left when I asked him. Tom picked up the left rein and tipped the colt's head to the left until his hindquarters stepped to the right. We did this several times and then Tom asked me to try moving him out again and to be real sensitive to when the colt was preparing to go right, and just then for me to reach down on that left rein, tip the colt's head left pretty firmly so his hindquarters would step right, and then continue to move in the direction we'd started. I had to try this a few times before my timing was accurate enough to catch the colt before his body was committed to the right turn, but soon we were headed right out and down the field. Next Tom had me trying again to trot the horse out in a big figure eight, and all I'd have to do was touch that left rein, and bring my left leg in, and the colt would prepare and position his body to go left.

Tom felt this was enough for the colt for that day, and as I went to put him up, Tom asked, "Oh, how is his trot feeling now?" I realized that it had been perfectly comfortable—it had taken care of itself while we worked on freeing up all of these other moves. So once again, without saying it, Tom had given me an old lesson over—it is never the "big thing" that we should focus on, but all the little things that come before that big thing, and then the big thing will take care of itself.

We worked on another mare that day and this was equally exciting. This was a twelve-year-old mare who was the first horse I had ever tried to start using Ray and Tom's ideas. She is a mare with a great disposition—willing to do whatever you want as long as she can figure out what it is. With me riding, that isn't always easy to do. One thing we had never gotten together on was picking up her right lead. She was very left handed and for the most part I just left it alone because I knew I didn't know how to fix it up. If we had to chase a cow or something, she would make her lead changes, but if I asked her to pick up a right lead in an arena, it was a disaster.

Just recently I had tried to work a little on this because my daughter was just starting to ride the mare in some walk-jog classes, and I knew the mare had to get handy on leads for pleasure classes in the future. For the first time in her life, the mare began to get bothered. I'd try to shorten my support rein and push on her leading side to extend and really push her into the lead. Sometimes we were successful, but in a very clumsy and frustrated way. In the meantime, the mare had gotten to where she was trying to beat me to the punch. When I asked her to trot and began to prepare her to take the right lead, she would speed up right away and push into a dead run on the left lead. Hardly what I had in mind for a child's pleasure class!

First, Tom had me work on just getting the mare with me again at a walk and trot in a straight line down the field. When she felt like she was staying with me, he asked me to take her in a big circle at a walk or trot. He said, "Don't try to lope, but don't worry about it if she does roll over into a lope; just keep her in this big right circle." Of course, I told him she would no doubt pick up the left lead if she went into the lope, but he said again not to *worry* about it if she did at this stage, but just to ride her through the lope and back to a trot.

Halfway around the first circle she rolled over, very relaxed, into a lope on the *right* side. I couldn't believe it! Tom just laughed and said she couldn't help but pick up that lead because her body had been so prepared for it. I still hadn't really felt it though, so we went back to the trot, and while I was trying to feel her "corners" and understand what the horse had to do to prepare to take a lead, she rolled over again onto the right lead. Now I was sure I had it and this time when I felt her body was positioned I tried to ask her for the lead. In an instant she repositioned herself and took the left lead. Ten more tries, ten more failures. Each time Tom would say, "Oh, just another stride or two and she would have had it." And so each time I'd try to wait for those couple of extra strides, and when everything felt just right I'd start to move her up to a lope and she'd switch and take the left lead.

After letting me work at this for a while, Tom called me over to visit. He said he noticed that everything would look just right until the last instant when I'd ask for the lope, and then the mare's head would tip right and she'd reach with her left hindquarter and move into the left lead. He suggested that I try just keeping her in a trot—using my leading (inside or right) leg to ask her right front leg to reach out, my supporting (outside or left) leg to keep the left hindquartrs from reaching and my supporting rein to shorten up that whole left side by *slightly* tipping her head left. So this time we just kind of rocked back and forth. We'd trot with her body in a good right arc, and as she would begin to speed up and lose that arc I would use my left side to shape her up again and then she would slow up a bit. After going around the circle maybe two or three times like this, she began keeping the right arc. Finally, just as naturally as if I weren't on her at all and she was just running free, she just rolled over into the lope on the right lead! What an exhilirating feeling! Tom shared my excitement. He seemed so happy for me and the mare—happy that I had felt what I needed to be able to feel and could get out of the mare's way so that she didn't have to fight against me, and happy for the mare that she didn't have to feel bothered but could fit my idea to become her idea and be so comfortable.

It must have been days before I was walking on the ground again after that experience. At times since then I've felt almost frantic in the fear that I'll forget the feel I experienced with the horses that day and will totally revert to some of my former bungling with them. I don't always succeed at achieving the level of togetherness I felt that day as I worked with these horses, though by and large things have continued to progress fairly well. When something doesn't work out just the way I planned, I've usually been able to stop and think about the situation and come to some of the basic principles that came through me: What are the little things that need attending to here so that the big movement can occur? How can I get out of the horse's way so he won't be bothered and can let my idea become his idea? I'm spending a lot more energy these days trying to look at the situation from the horse's point of view and to understand what the horse feels and thinks. To me, this is really the Tom Dorrance way.

—o—

When Tom was up to the ranch he worked with us and our horses on the ditch bank. He took us up to the ditch bank and taught us how to get the horse to rate off and use his hind legs while he was coming down. In other words, we went down the hill and across the ditch repeatedly until the saddle leveled up; that was an indication that the horse was really putting his hind legs under him.

Stop the horse and let him back out. We learned that just after you break over the hill, if you block the forward motion and the avenue to the right or the left, the horse himself will soon back straight up the hill and out, thereby teaching the horse how to use his hind legs. It gets him to where he is not afraid to stop because he knows he can do it easily. It really helped our horses and it helped us.

Until he puts his hind legs under him, the saddle will be steep, but as soon as he levels off, gets his hind legs down under him, then your saddle levels out.

This is, I'm sure, what Tom was watching for before he would stop us and have us back the horse out. I'm sure the object of it was for the horse to find his way out of the steep hill backwards without any help from us—do you see what I mean?

It helped tremendously to get the horse to stop properly when we were in the arena later. He would tell us—the horse would tell us that he was ready to stop—after this.

Later a friend called and we were discussing, on the phone, different problems, and I told him what Tom had done for us with these horses that were stopping real peggy. His horse was pegging when he stopped, instead of putting his hind feet under him and balancing to a balanced stop. I talked to him later and he said it really worked wonderfully for him.

Most important though: the one thing that has helped me more than anything else that I have learned from Tom is to set it up and wait. If you know what I mean. I use it all the time and it's done me more good than anything. If you can just learn to set it up and wait; and I think the main thing is the waiting part of it. Of course you have to set it up right. If you set it up too harsh then you have to wait longer for it. Do it easier and you don't have to wait long for it to come right through.

As long as you are working with the horse there is going to be a certain amount of frustration. You get flustered over this one because he won't go to the left—everything you have ever tried on every horse ahead of this guy has worked but it won't work on this guy.

So you are flustered! And if you can just think back—stop and remember—close your eyes or whatever it takes—*wait*.

You know, just set it up and wait—set it up and wait—pretty soon it's going to come through, and when it does it just comes through so nice. I think about it often; every time I saddle up I make myself use it. If I'm going to set up for a nice pivot over here—back up or whatever I'm going to do—if I'm walking my horse ahead and I want him to stop and come right out of that stop into a backward motion—I just wait. If

I ask for it real sharp there's resentment there, and it takes longer to get it. You've passed it—you go through it.

There's a spot there. If you work on this soft, easy, nice little spot, just everything works good, but if you get too anxious and go beyond—on through that spot—you have nothing. Oh, you have something all right but it's not what you want. You know it's not right. So, then you have to either unsaddle or get off and recinch your saddle, or walk around, or do something.

Then start this thing over again.

—o—

You need to learn to go with the horse so you can get the horse to come with you. If you just put it into a few words that's all there is to horsemanship, is for you to get with the horse so the horse has an opportunity to learn to get with your feel so you both go together. But it is hard to apply because you have to adjust while you are getting the horse to adjust. The horse learns fairly soon if the person who is handling him understands the mental makeup of the horse. You have to understand them mentally first. Then you understand what they are capable of doing physically. But they learn fairly fast if the person that's handling them understands, and of course that's the slow part because for the person that is handling the horse there is so much more to learn. They've got so many things they are adjusting to all the time, even to one horse, because that horse is adjusting mentally. He is adjusting, so you have to adjust with him, to get him to adjust to you. And the feel you offer him, it's from the very softest feel you can possibly offer him, to your full strength under some cases. So you have to learn how much firmness to use. And that's your timing. You might be hitting it pretty close; you might be about as close as you'd get with the feel you were offering the horse, but if you are out of time with it then it wouldn't be developing satisfactorily. But, if your timing was right when your feel was good of the horse, then the horse has a far better opportunity with you, some sooner than others (*of course*).

There are so many little things that will hold a horse up—that will bother him—especially a young horse that hasn't been handled too much. He may be skeptical or something; those spots a horse is bothered about are the ones you kind of want to work on.

If you just want to put it in as few words as possible, why all there is to it is learning to feel of the horse and then teaching him to feel you. But it takes a long time because there are so many things to learn. It's like knowing when the opportunity is there to present a horse with feel. There are so many opportunities after you get a mental picture of what things do. Then you have to get yourself into the habit of doing them when the opportunity is there. A lot of times the opportunity is there when you are just going along, to do a little something for your horse, and it doesn't tire your horse or anything—but the rider may think the horse was going along all right and there wasn't any reason to turn him this way or stop him, or any reason to trot him up there a bit or maybe ride him over this way a little out of the trail. The rider might think there wasn't any reason to do this since the horse was going along more or less relaxed. But there is a real reason to do it! An opportunity to get the horse prepared to do something that will be real necessary in the future, so the horse will be familiar with going with your feel to get your job done.

I find it takes quite a little while for a person to get into the habit of doing that. Especially if they are alone a lot. If they've got somebody to talk to, somebody maybe a little more advanced than they are, it is a big help.

One thing that helped me a lot: one time I was riding colts and I had a lot of young horses to ride and I didn't have time to ride all of them. Tom had some slack time in Oregon that summer, and he came down to help me. He was there maybe six weeks or so. Most of the colts were six or seven years old. They had all been halter broke but that was about all. I really wasn't with those horses like I needed to be.

One day I was riding a mare that was a good moving animal; she traveled real free and her feet were in under her. Tom was riding a horse that took a big old long step—then he took another step. He was kind of a long horse anyway and every time he put his foot down, it just went down *kerplunk*. This mare didn't step too far and picked her feet up quick-smooth. The horse Tom was riding just went along there kind of one step at a time and was reaching way out. He was walking about as fast as she was, but he was rough.

Tom told me there is such a difference in the feel of these two horses. He said, "This horse here, he'd be a lot easier to get with than that mare you are riding." "Well," I said, "let's trade horses, then." So I got on that horse.

He said you could feel the difference in those horses. I had been in the army so I got to counting with his feet. I tried to count one-two-three-four, and I hit it part of the time, but I finally found out if I just concentrated on one front foot and shut my eyes so there were no distractions at all, then I could feel that foot come up. At first I just felt it hit the ground. Then pretty soon I got so I could feel it when it was coming up and then that was the time to direct it (when it was coming up) and get the feel there just when it's ready to leave the ground.

That gave me a big start right there. Then right after that there was a girl visiting at the ranch. She really liked to ride. She was kind of short and a little bit chubby, but when she was on the horse she just went along, just a part of the horse. I'd been riding the colts around there. She liked to go out and ride if there was anybody going out on horseback.

One day we were out riding. I was riding a colt, and he wasn't too soft. He was liable to do something most any time, take off or something. So I was sitting on him kind of braced.

For something to talk about she said something about she'd been to riding school in Washington. So I asked her what were some of the things they taught at the riding school.

She said they taught them how to kind of stay out from under a horse's feet, and get on them and off of them—put the bridle and saddle on them and things like that—then she said they taught them what the better posture was on a horse.

Well, I hadn't heard anybody say anything about posture on a horse before. I didn't have it. I was sitting there with kind of a brace on that horse because I didn't know but what he might take off any time. I was sitting there with my hips pushed back against the cantle of the saddle a little bit and my feet were pushed out a little, which wasn't the right way to sit on a horse.

I thought a little bit. Then I asked her, "What is better posture on a horse?" She kind of talked about something else. I didn't think too much about that. See, I didn't have it, and she was a person who didn't want to offend anybody.

So pretty soon I got to thinking about it a little more. I thought, maybe, she hadn't heard me. She was real friendly, so I asked her again. She kinda smiled a little bit and pretty soon she was talking about something else. So I could see for some reason—I didn't know why—she wasn't wanting to talk about what better posture on a horse was. In a little bit I kind of put on a big smile and looked over at her and said, "For some reason or another you don't seem to want to talk about what the better posture is on a horse!"

So then she came out with a big smile and she said, "Well, it's just like you are when you are standing—your shoulders are balanced on your hips and your feet are in under you and they are just pressing down in the stirrups to a certain extent. You are just lined up all the way through your body—you are balanced all the way through—there is a curve in your back forward."

Well! That sounded good. No doubt I rode that way when I first started to ride. I got to looking at other people who hadn't been riding. Most little kids will sit up straight, sit relaxed on a horse if they aren't afraid. So I went to watching people.

When I got better posture again on a horse I found how important it was to teach those horses to feel of your legs, because my legs were down there free then; they didn't have a brace in them. I didn't have to use my quirt so much, and I didn't have to pull on them so much because my legs were there to support my arms.

Then other times when Tom would come down we'd visit, but it was hard for Tom and me to get together when we were visiting because he was visiting up where he'd be doing it, and I needed to be talking down below, but I didn't know where to start down there. That spot down there was where I needed to start—I didn't know where it was.

Tom could take a horse and start at the top speed and work down on him if it was necessary. Or he'd start down and work up. But if it were necessary to go fast, he could speed that horse up to get the job done, and he'd teach the horse to feel of him when he was speeded up, and then gradually slow him down. But you've got to be experienced to do that—and I wasn't that far along.

Finally I learned to stay out of the horse's way, and I didn't interfere with him too much, and I went with him a lot—but I can look back and see how much better the horse could have been if I'd have gotten with him.

It's real interesting to look back. I can see I've made about all the mistakes I've seen anybody else make, and I can understand why it's happening like it is.

It makes me think it would have been fortunate to have had that knowledge when I had my youth. Life is in some ways too short. I don't know of anybody that's teaching this much.

The most natural thing for most people with a problem is to force the issue. They think they've got to. You'll see when the rider doesn't present the horse at the right time with quite the right feel—then you'll see how things don't work. The person that has the most understanding when these things show up—they don't try to force it. They'll ease off and take a new start instead of trying to force the issue. Some people think if they ease off on the horse the horse will get to quitting and he won't try. Well, if they didn't have anything to offer the horse after they did ease off likely that's what the horse would do. It would be just like the young colt they were riding and he was kind of set on going over to the corral where the other horses were. Every time they came by that spot, if the rider just eased off and let him go over there, never did anything else and never had anything else to offer, pretty soon that's all he'd think about doing. But if you would present a feel to him that he would understand and be responsive to, even if there was something attracting his attention, he'd still feel of you and go where your body was lined up to go.

Tom always claimed he learned more by trying to help somebody than he ever learned otherwise—there is a lot of truth in that. You do learn by helping others, because if they are getting to the point where they can progress a little bit, then you are getting a pretty good picture over to them, and if you don't, they aren't going to see it. So, if you aren't getting something over to them that they are capable of handling, then you have to back off and figure out another different little thing you can put in there so they can make use of it.

I was forty years old before I found out how important some of these other things are. Now I can see so many people in that same spot. Everybody was doing the best they could but by not having enough understanding the most natural thing to do was to put the horse under more pressure. A few horses would take that and stay out of the rider's way; they were the ones that made the good horses because they beat the guy to it. When they felt the pressure coming on, they'd start to move to get away from it—not to run off or something—but they'd get moving in the direction the fellow wanted to move, because if they didn't, the fellow would keep pulling on them and get them all pulled out of balance.

One thing a less experienced rider might not be working on is when they start a horse out they may not be aware to line their body toward a certain place. Those young horses, if you don't do that, they don't have enough feel there to get hooked onto. It takes them a while to get hooked on anyway, even if a person is experienced. But you have to keep offering that to them—many times you line your body up toward something and ride your horse in that direction, and after a while those horses get so they stay right under you—it doesn't matter where you line your body up to. You don't have to use your reins any to speak of, and they'll stay right under you.

I got that from Tom. He was responsible for my getting it, but he didn't tell me what to do. He told me to look out there toward something, but he didn't tell me what I had to do with the rest of my body. I'd look out there, but the horse he'd still be kind of weaving. But I wasn't giving him enough leg support. I was sitting on the horse too still. Even if he was a free traveling horse, he'd still get to weaving. When I got so my body feel was really getting with that horse—then helping a little with my legs—the horse got to feeling of me. Then wherever my body was lined up to go the horse stayed right under it. Colts, any of them, will twist and squirm around on you to start with because they don't know about it—but in time they'll get so you can just line up and go.

If I were going to start out to write a book where I'd start would be to try to explain how you need to feel of a horse when they are moving. That's what I like to do when I go to help anybody if I can. We may start a little bit on something else that they are real interested in, but I like to wind up down there to get them with that horse's feet.

First off, sometimes the rider doesn't have the horse taught to stand when he gets on him; or he isn't taught to stand after the rider gets on. Lots of times the rider is active enough so that the horse can be stepping off and the rider can just step on as the horse is moving on. *But* if you miss that spot, the horse isn't learning to wait for you, and *he isn't learning to feel of you.*

Catching a horse can be a problem for lots of folks. You know a horse doesn't like to be followed if he can't get away; he doesn't like it. If he starts to go, just let him go and kind of help him go. Pretty soon he'll find out that's not so good.

If a horse doesn't feel right, his feet are either hung up or he can be in a wrong position to take a step or something like that; or else he isn't willing. That can be in there just as much as anything. If the horse isn't willing to do something then you've gotta help him in an understanding way to get in the mood to do something.

As I was traveling a little better with those horses, that gave me a lot better feel. As I got more to offer the horse, he was less apt to buck with me because I was with him and he didn't get lost like he did before, because I had a good feel to offer him and was up there moving with him.

I got the idea from Tom, too, about working their heads around there. You can't do too much of that. Some people say all you are doing is making them rubber necked. That is all you are doing if you don't have anything else to go with it. No! You'd better leave his neck stiff out there so he can use it for a pry then. You need the horse to be soft all the way through. You are riding the horse as a whole feel. Until a person gets so he can do that it's liable to be too much of a hit and miss deal.

—o—

It's really hard for me to put it into words, what I've gotten from Tom. I did sit down and write some things one night and then after I read it, I wasn't very pleased.

I had never really worked with Tom until these last clinics. I had heard lots of Tom Dorrance stories from Bryan and other guys, and I have had help from them. I've had help from Bill too. I first heard about Tom from Ray Hunt. Back then there weren't many guys to talk about working with horses, this way. Now I run into people all the time who have met Tom or Ray, and they are working for some of these things in their horses.

It's real hard—I don't believe anyone will ever really get it all. I don't think there'll be another Tom Dorrance, but I do think he's made it a lot easier on a lotta horses. Take just loading horses; just about anybody that's been around this has so much less problem in that one area.

Tom just sees so much of what's inside the horse—how the horse feels and thinks. In so many little ways he is really looking out for the horse.

When I went to that first clinic with my roan horse, one of the first things Tom pointed out to me was how bothered my horse was inside. I knew he got bothered, but I didn't realize I could be bothering him.

After Tom worked with me that day, the horse really let down. He was really with me. What we had there, that day, felt real good. I wish I could say we have it at home now, but I haven't yet got it as good as it was that day.

I want to have him trust me and want to be with me. I'm not sure yet how to get it—I don't know where I'm missing.

I've got some colts at home I'm riding. They run together in a pasture, and I wrangle them in the mornings. I grain them but still it seems like they'd rather not be with me.

This week I'm working away from home so I've hauled them up to these corrals where I'm staying. They sure have a different relationship with me up there. Seems like they are real glad to see me. Maybe they feel more dependent on me. I like their attitude better. I'd like to get that in my horses. I'd like to get that from my roan horse. Maybe if I could get that, I could get this other, I don't know.

In the clinic I learned something about myself when Tom had me riding. When he had me picture where I was going and just line out and go, the horse's ears came forward. He felt good. But one time around, one of the other horses sort of put his ears back. My horse was bothered. I didn't pay much attention to it and the next time around the problem really surfaced. Tom called me over and pointed out to me how my horse had tried to tell me the time before that there was a real problem there. I just wasn't listening close enough to my horse. I don't know how many times a person misses things like that, when the horse is telling you and you don't listen. I'm really trying to learn from my horses. I'm hoping I'll get another chance to be around Tom pretty soon.

—o—

Oh my, where do I start? How can anyone put into words what it is like to work with Tom?

To me, he is the most amazing person I have ever had the pleasure to know. He works magic with horses.

I have been fortunate enough to watch Tom with a few different horses and see a whole new personality develop in the horse: one that is instantly calm, relaxed and trusting. They seem to instantly know that here is some rare individual of the human race that understands them and why they respond the way they do, whether or not it is right or wrong in "our" book of rules.

It is so much *fun* to ride or just be around horses after working with Tom. Of course anything that stimulates the brain is exciting—and that is exactly what it is to work with Tom. You have to think and learn to think like a horse!

I always seem to feel a little frustrated after I've been to a clinic or to Tom's. I feel as if I've been completely wrong about what Tom has meant to get across to me. But after a few days back home, riding and feeling and thinking, I feel better and have a little more understanding of the horses and why they do the things they do.

To be more and more like Tom Dorrance is a goal I plan to work for during my lifetime—to understand horses so well and to have their respect.

—o—

I am not very good at writing and probably worse on words.

There are many things that Tom has helped me with, such as being more aware of the horse, trying to understand what he is thinking.

One thing he really made me aware of is realizing if the horse is left or right handed. This has really helped me get my horses stronger on the right.

Tom has helped me with getting just a little roll in the hindquarters. This has really helped my horses get softer on all four corners. I have better luck getting a little roll in the hindquarters than I do if I rein the hind quarters too far around. It seems like some horses, you can rein their hindquarters around all day and as soon as you straighten out he is stiff again—so I have real good luck with asking for a little roll; let him go a little ways and ask for a little roll again. Pretty soon you just think about asking for the roll and it's there. The roll may only be an inch or more, but I think it's a little thing that softens up your whole horse.

Another thing that Tom helped me with is straightness in the horse. This is probably one of the most important things. I'm not saying I can do it all the time, but I am a lot more aware of it. This fits in with being a right or left handed horse; if he's strong on the left he's not going to be straight, or vice versa.

One time Tom helped me with a horse that had been on the open range all his life and had never been touched by human hands. Anyway, we got him in the round corral and Tom told me exactly what spot in the corral I was to rope him because any other spot would have probably made him jump out. I got him caught, and Tom had me just follow him around and around until I got close enough to reach out and touch him; he would just keep right on walking along like nothing was wrong. But if I reached out to touch him at the wrong time, he would jump about ten feet and get upset. This is something that is not real clear to me, and I would like some more work with this sort of thing.

Another thing I'm not real sure of, is Tom helped me with another horse that he said kept throwing me slack. Anyway, before this I always thought that when a horse gave you slack you'd give slack back to him. But this horse, when I was backing him, would throw me slack *so he could call the shots.* This is something I would like more help on also.

Another thing that I would like to hear more about is the first few rides on a horse when you're riding him around. I hear Tom say support him when he gets to this spot, or support him when he goes by there. I'd like to hear more on this, on the idea of what you do that supports him. I think I have maybe 80 percent of this support thing figured out.

Also, I would like to understand more on how to get a horse to prepare to position.

—o—

Several years ago a friend of Tom's said, "It seems like Tom knows what an animal is going to do before the animal has thought of doing it. Years later when Tom was asked if he could explain this, he said it was just the way you approach to get the unity that is desired. Well, that was a simple answer, the person said, but it still is confusing if the approach isn't understood.

"OK," Tom said, "you see those five head of cattle lying down over there on that little knoll [about an eighth of a mile]? The cattle look comfortable and satisfied, so we will see if we can ride that way and not disturb them. As we approach, when we get closer we will pick one of the five; then as we continue our approach, we will watch real closely and try to arrange our approach so that one we have picked will get up first and walk over toward that little bush."

It worked, and Tom asked, "Does that answer your question? It isn't that I know what they are going to do before they thought of it—it is a matter of me *thinking first—then arranging my approach so that my idea will become their idea.*" It is so simple it is difficult for a person to understand. Again it is the little things that make the big difference. They are so important, these things. It takes feel and timing to get the balance that is needed.

So many times a person may say, "I didn't see Tom do anything. Why did it happen?"

I have heard Tom say, "I believe this has to come right out of the inside of a person in order for it to come from the inside of the animal." Again, I will say it is the little things that make the big difference. A person must think of the animal first—then start at zero. I believe it is from zero to one where the problems start.

Tom has told me many times in visiting with someone in person or by telephone about their horse problems, it is much easier for him to help them if they have been to one or more of Ray Hunt's clinics. After listening to their stories it seems they can be so close to getting results but just not quite getting it all together. When he asks them if they remember hearing Ray mention *the importance of watching for the smallest change and slightest try*, so many times that is all Tom has to say. Ray had presented it to them; now all they needed was *to let it penetrate.*

—o—

The most important thing is the softness and how to recognize this. I've probably missed more than anybody. It all goes with asking the horse and being ready to give to him. It just boils down to taking the horse for what he is, for his athletic ability and other abilities too. I think it has been a real good lesson in common sense.

There's another thing I would like to add. It has been almost twenty-five years since I was first around Tom and I sometimes wonder if I'm just now beginning to get the benefit of what I saw and I sometimes wonder if I've even scratched the surface.

—o—

This is a story of what I saw take place at a barbecue one evening at one of Ray Hunt's clinics. We had just gotten seated and started to eat when a young cat showed up and was quite interested in the event. Someone reached to pick up the cat to take it out of the shed. At this instant the cat jumped up on Tom's lap. Tom seemed to hardly notice the cat was there. He just lowered his elbow easy and smooth-like and drew the cat close to his side and continued to visit with those beside him and eat his supper as though the cat were not there. The cat looked a little surprised, but was not scared. It didn't try to escape; it just sort of looked around for a minute. It seemed to be comfortable but started to show signs of maybe getting a little uneasy with the confinement.

When the cat would start to move as if to leave Tom would apply just enough pressure so the cat would withdraw and settle down. This went on for a few minutes. Each time the cat would put a little more effort into trying to escape but would feel the pressure increasing to compensate for its effort to escape. Tom didn't act as if he knew the cat was there.

After the cat had made several attempts to escape, it just stayed real quiet but was looking as if it was going to really do something about getting free. Then all of a sudden it made the big effort—and there was no resistance from Tom. It was perfect timing. The cat had gotten the message. It left the building, not scared but real business-like, and was not seen the rest of the evening.

—o—

When I first heard of Tom, I could not imagine him living up to his reputation and still be human. I was about half scared to even let him know I was around. I was told he knew what a person was thinking before they thought it, and that bothered me. But after I got to know him personally, I found that he had a good sense of humor and was a lot of fun to work around.

I had been exposed to this philosophy by Ray fairly young, and being raised on a ranch I had had enough bad experiences with horses. I really appreciated an easier way to get the job done.

I think a lot of people who have been exposed to this philosophy work their horses with these ideas but pass up a lot of opportunities with cattle and other animals. I have found if I can keep myself in the frame of mind that Tom keeps his horses in, I am a lot more comfortable. When my temper would get in my way and I would get frustrated, I could just back off and think about what was happening, then go into it a little slower. I could stay in control, and the job would be easier, the same way it is with horses.

One day Tom was over to my house and we were working with some horses, and we stopped for a few minutes and were talking. My two young boys, two and three years old, wanted to play with Tom while we were trying to visit. They were on the verge of being a nuisance, and I suggested to them that they leave, but Tom said that they were all right. Then I noticed that Tom kept pointing his finger at their chest when they would try to get close to him, and he never broke his conversation with me. The boys kept trying to wrestle with him, but all they could get to was his finger. So they grabbed it, and Tom would tug them a little and pull away, and they thought that was fun. When they got on to his game they weren't any nuisance at all. They were right there under control where we could keep an eye on them. They were having fun, and they were not disturbing us at all.

When I was in high school, I started a lot of colts through the winters and feel that I came a long way, looking back at the before and after. At the same time, I was trying to relate to people around me in the same way, with next-to-nothing for results. So I just put that on the shelf for a while, and in time it came to me—I was trying to work with an "old dog" the way you would relate to a puppy. I was trying to compare a fresh colt with an open mind to a person who was very much the opposite, being unreasonable, letting pride block the way and being overconfident with what they know.

Then after riding some horses that had been around and had learned to outthink people, instead of the person outthinking them, I had to learn a different way of approaching this type of horse. You couldn't just walk up to them with confidence and guts and pet them to let them know you wanted to be their friend; they had already learned not to trust a person, and some of them wanted to take advantage of me if they got the chance. It was tough for me to get this type of horse in a good frame of mind and then keep him there while I approached him with something that he would relate to the past. At the time, all I could relate to was: "make the wrong thing difficult and the right thing easy," and I might win the battle but I wouldn't always win the war. Looking back, it was really crude, the way I went about it sometimes, but the horses always seemed to forgive me in time. I learned a lot from this type of horse, and I still do because they really make me pay attention so I don't overlook little things.

Ray and Tom have pointed out things to me that I didn't think made any difference, or wasn't even aware of. A lot of times some of the smallest things would make all the difference in how things turned out.

Then I realized that this is the way some people are. You have to watch for the smallest things, but at the same time, stay relaxed and don't make them uncomfortable; just like a horse that has his mind made up. A lot of times the person may be set in his ways, which I don't think is all bad. They will have some good in there somewhere, if you look, and you can build a relationship from there.

One of the problems that Tom helped me with recently is getting on a colt the first time. I never gave it much thought when I got on a horse, as long as they didn't try to leave before I was "on" and "ready." If they needed to take a step or so, I thought that was all right. I knew I had a small problem from time to time getting off, and if the horse didn't take care of it himself, it usually got worse before it got better, but I never associated it with getting on.

One day I stepped onto a colt and he moved a step to steady himself, and Tom pointed out to me that the colt wasn't ready for my weight. So, he told me how to get the horse ready for my weight by pulling on the saddle, and soon the horse would plant his feet and stand as solid as a statue.

Then when I got on and rode him around and he felt my weight go to the left stirrup after I stopped him, he would brace himself like he was holding a cow on the end of a rope. I would step off, lead him out of his tracks, and get ready to get on again, and he would get ready when he felt my weight pull the saddle; I could feel him pull against it. His feet really got solid mounting and dismounting, yet I could move him with my legs and reins after I got on him, the same as always.

—o—

During the past three years I've had an opportunity to spend quite a lot of time with Tom.

I had gotten in kind of deep, and didn't look like I would get out. Tom gave me the help I needed and I began to look at the horse a lot different. It was a real attitude adjustment for me as far as the horse was concerned.

Tom made me aware of the little things that are so important to the horse and to listen to what the horse was telling me.

Some of the horses we were working with were real bothered and had some real problems built in them.

Things just didn't happen overnight, and I couldn't see the forest for the trees for a while, but Tom paints a good picture and things started to fall in place.

Some of the horses really put themselves through a lot before they got confidence in themselves; once they got that confidence they began to have confidence in us. Even with Tom's help it took me a long time to see what was needed for the horse and to see the changes taking place within the horse that give one the answers. I am by no means there yet, but I am a lot more aware of what's taking place within the horse and am more concerned with his feelings.

The approach, feel and timing is so important that if it is missed, it might be better if you hadn't started.

This third factor that Tom speaks of (Spirit) is that which has to come from within. It's a feel that is very hard to explain but means so much to the horse. As Tom explains it, if a person attains this, then loses it, it will probably never fully be regained with that particular horse. The best way I can think of to explain this is a feel between you and the horse of complete trust and confidence in one another, with no drag.

I was first aware of this when Tom had been helping me for sometime with this horse we called Roanie. Roanie was real bothered and would just as soon have been somewhere else, he was really panicked. But when he started to get confidence in himself, and began to look towards us for help and security, I began to be aware of this factor Tom was talking about.

I was leading him back to the barn one night with just a lariat rope around his neck; it was about fifty feet long, and ole Roanie could be out on the end of it somewhere in between or right next to me. He wasn't bothered at all like he had been. It also felt like I wouldn't have needed the rope to direct him. I was aware of this again with another horse that I started on the first ride. So I know it can be. I think some people have worked in this area, but are not aware of it.

A fellow once said that he had no problem in working with a horse from one to ten but it was from zero to one where the problem is. It's the little things that are the most important and often missed or forgotten that make the difference. Straightness in a horse, having him be on all four corners, that's what is taking place in a horse inside. It's working at the level of where the horse is at, so he can understand what is being offered.

These are some of the things Tom has made me aware of. My sincere thanks to Tom, my good friend, for putting a little light in the tunnel.

—o—

Editorial Note

One of the fellows Tom has been helping insists this book should be as big as a stack of Sears Roebuck catalogues. Likely, that whole stack would not hold all the stories riders could tell of the ways Tom has helped them understand and overcome a particular problem with their horses, and the ways working with him has changed their attitude about their horses.

A lifetime of learning from horses cannot be compressed into one small book. Many horses' lifetimes could be enriched, however, if the rider could put to use one small sentence from the first chapter of this book: *"The rider need to recognize the horse's need for self-preservation in mind, body and spirit."*

A whole stack of large volumes would be of no value to the rider who fails to recognize and meet these needs for his horse.

Tom's basic beliefs were introduced to the reader in the first three sections: "Feel the Whole Horse," "Responsive and Right On," and "Approach and Unity."

In "Feel the Whole Horse," Tom says, "I try to feel what the horse is feeling and operate from where the horse is." The simplicity of this statement may cause the reader to read over it in search of *important concepts.* The rider who can recognize and apply this one important concept could fill volumes with accounts of what was learned from these experiences.

We are more concerned in this work with recognizing and applying the philosophy than with filling volumes. As you read the following section, "Learning to Do Less to Get More," try to recognize in these experiences the philosophy in action.

Visualize approaching the horse with an attitude of total acceptance, where any action or response from the horse will be met with understanding.

Listen for the times the rider is encouraged to direct and support the horse.

Watch for the confidence the horse has built up in the person, which is so easy to destroy.

See the care that is used, so as not to destroy this closeness between the horse and the rider.

Picture the rider arranging a learning situation so the horse comes into his own pressure rather than the rider putting pressure on the horse.

Think of working through any problem or learning situation in an atmosphere of togetherness between the horse and rider.

Recognize what is taking place in any situation to cause it to be good or not so good.

Learn to help the horse get into a position that will come out better.

Learn to help the horse avoid getting into a position that's not so good.

Realize that what doesn't fit between the horse and the rider often gets blamed on the horse. The rider can be unaware the horse is doing just what the rider has trained the horse to do.

So many vital concepts were introduced in the first three chapters— only a few of them have been emphasized here. The reader will be able to recognize these and many more in the following pages.

Learning to Do Less to Get More

Once when I was helping some riders, one rider commented: "In a way I feel like I haven't gotten much going. Usually you can't see that much progress with the horse, but at the same time I feel like I can recognize all the basic crookedness, at least. Sometimes I don't do the right thing to fix them but I am learning."

I had been working with this rider a little now and then for several years. She was beginning to figure out what she was missing and to be able to make things more interesting and rewarding for herself and the horse.

What she was doing that day gets to be the main part of riding. Soon, the rider will feel more of these parts where the horse needs help, and the rider will be able to help the horse more on them. This makes a big difference as to how the horse gets to shaping up. The horse will get to working better with just a little help.

This rider was learning along with the horse. Part of what she was saying was there were times when things happened before she recognized that was the way it was going to turn out. Then, if it kept happening she would begin to search for a way to help the horse. That is where this rider was operating at this time, and it looked good—*real good.*

I had wanted to visit with the rider about this; that is the reason I had asked her to pull in from the ride. I didn't want her to miss thinking about what she was doing. I was pretty sure the rider knew what she was doing, but I wanted to stress the importance of what she was doing.

She was helping the horse shape up when the horse was cantering. As the horse was elevating all she would have to do was steady him (that looked good). I call that playing the tune, and she was doing that. It is something they have to learn. There are other things the rider can do that will help them lead up to it, but the person has to really feel of the horse. The rider has to feel everything about the horse—front, back, inside and outside—in order to do that, because if they are not feeling that, they have no idea what to do. They may know the horse isn't feeling right, is not operating right, but the rider doesn't know what to do to help him.

The horse needs to get his feet and legs and their joints and muscles going so they can be prepared. When the horse gets to the time when he needs to be in position, he can be in position all the way through, instead of just part of him.

Sometimes, that one part is *pretty good*, but the rest of the horse doesn't complement the good part. Say they are in position for the right bend when you ask them for the left bend; if they don't get in position for that transition, they can't make the proper bend. These are things a person needs to get to thinking about. The rider may be thinking about the bend, but not thinking about preparing for it. The rider isn't thinking of preparing for the transition, or thinking of stopping. He is not thinking of the horse needing to learn how to prepare to position for the transition. A transition can be going from a walk to a trot, going from a trot to canter, canter to run, or just right back down, or sidepass or whatever.

Sometimes if you see a horse doesn't have time to position for the transition you are working for, then you may go on around and take another try. If you feel you have time and if you have the chance to come through, you can hang in there quite a while and then sometimes right in the nth degree the horse will go and come through. The horse will start learning from there.

There was an example of that with the horse that was backing up toward the fence. When the horse got close to the fence he was going to have to go one way or the other. The horse was trying to position for the left, when he was being asked to position for the right. If we didn't watch it and he had any advantage at all, he was going to use that advantage to go to the left. It was important to have him positioned so it was going to be easier for him to yield to the right. These are some of the things that are important in preparing for the feel of the whole horse, not only where his feet and legs are but all through the horse and where he needs the help. You try to help him in those areas without taking the good away.

Sometimes when I am helping a rider I will have him trot the horse out and make some curves, and I'll watch. When he is trotting out there *the rider* is picking the course ahead, quite a little ways out there, where he wants the horse to go. Then the rider will try to get the horse's attention on that imaginery line. (The rider may be already caught up on this.)

It isn't really an imaginary line—*it is real*, if you have it picked. There is nothing there but it's just as real as if it were a big broad white line (after it gets to working for the horse and the rider). The rider picks the line and to start with, the horse isn't going to know where it is, even though the rider has it picked. That is where the rider's body and everything is wanting to go, *but the rider doesn't go without the horse.* The horse may drift from that line some if he needs the room to drift, but pretty soon he will get right on that line that has been picked, and he won't want to be anywhere else but where the rider is.

At first the horse may be ready to go somewhere, but he won't know where. He may be exploring, looking around. It won't be very long until when the rider prepares to leave, the horse will know right where the rider is going, and will go right where he is looking. It will be interesting for the horse and he will have something to look forward to. He will get a lot more steady and secure about things.

Another thing that often happens is that the rider will be set to go to the left. Ninety-five percent of the time that is where people start: *to the left*, and 95 percent of the horses operate better to the left than they do to the right. (I'm just picking that percent figure out of the air. It could be more like 98 percent.)

I like to have the rider try to be opposite to what generally takes place. I want them to start out to the right, then if they only get this one round, the horse is exercised to the right. Now when a horse gets so he is not strong either to the right or to the left, *if he is balanced*, then it doesn't matter. All the rider will have to do, then, is watch that he doesn't start getting lopsided.

I was working with a rider who was having trouble getting the horse to stop the way the rider wanted. The rider said he would pick up a soft feel, then lose it, and *stop*—then the horse would get soft for the rider again. I had the rider go out and ride around just a little. The mare was good and even and not too bad on the curves. Sometimes, on getting the horse to stop smooth, the rider can get the horse to trotting, coming around pretty good, and then instead of asking the horse to stop straight (square) the rider comes into a little short circle, getting the horse to think about stopping. The rider just lets him think about stopping. Just *let* the horse find the stop—*don't try to make him stop.* The thing you are trying to do is to get him to thinking about stopping, then when he catches up on that, when you ask him to stop when you are going straight, he will be thinking about stopping instead of going on. Be especially careful not to have any pressure on when the horse comes in there going to stop. The reason I say to have all the pressure off when he comes down in there to stop is, if it isn't, he is going to take those extra steps. You are going to have ahold of him, and he will get to pushing on you. If he is going to stop and there is nothing there for him to get ahold of, he will just learn to stop when you ease off. Instead of pulling him in, you let him know you are wanting to stop; you will ease off. He will stop, and he won't have anything to push on.

Keep in mind it is a learning process, for the horse and for the rider.

You can use natural riding situations to help the horse learn. One rider asked about a horse that was all up front going along pounding his front feet. He was doing this going straight, not bringing enough drive from behind. The rider needed to work with him to get that life and drive from behind. I told the rider one of the things that would help get some drive in the back quarters was if she would ride the horse in the hills. You will go up steep places and you will encourage the horse to go straight so he gets ahold and pulls and drives. You will just get him to climbing with a little more energy in it. Then if you get more energy he has to use the whole self—*and he has to learn how!*

The same thing if you are coming down a steep place. Before you get to where it breaks over, you get the horse *straight* and you get him even. When he starts to break over, he will start preparing to bring those hind feet under him, stepping shorter in front and letting the back ones catch up under him and settle down, instead of tipping over. These are good exercises, up hill and down hill for the back quarters.

While working with a group of riders in Elko, Nevada, one fall, I saw that one fellow was having a little trouble with a young filly. She was having trouble lining out when he wanted to go somewhere. Right in the spot when he asked for just a little more drive, she wasn't doing too much. When the filly did change she just broke into a little choppy trot—instead of getting with it and reaching. The filly looked like it would be so easy for her to get with it and just tick right along, but she got down into this slump.

What I am trying to point out is that a horse like this has lots of ability. It is just a matter of being able to bring the best out in a horse, because there is so much more she could do. It's all there, but it needs help to bring it out.

The rider had been trying to get this to come through, but it had been just sort of hanging. The thing was to try to get the filly to operating, walking right out with interest and enjoying it.

Some horses will need to be allowed to trot for more strides than others. Others you can check them pretty early if they are inclined to want to go on. If one is inclined to want to chop off too quick then you try to encourage him to carry on a little longer before you ask him to come back to the walk. That depends on the horse. With this one, if she broke into the trot and you waited too long, she would just figure on trotting farther each time. On a horse that wants to chop off too quick, if you let him come back too early, then he would just keep chopping off that much quicker. With that horse, you would want to carry on further, while with the other one you would want to check a little early. I don't know if I'm making that too clear or not. You try to analyze the horse and what he needs and then work from there, instead of just going out there and trying to do the same thing with each individual horse. They are all different. You are trying to adjust to what the horse needs.

Then the question came up: "When they start to chopping in front, do you slow up or push them on?"

Again, there are times when you will do either, and you will use both for getting them to line out or slow down. Those front and back feet, they need to be thinking about each other. One end of the horse can feel pretty good, and the other end can feel like there isn't much going on back there. Or the back end is better than the front end. The front end isn't doing so good. So you can get the horse together. I used to speak of it as *you get so you can ride the two ends together*. The horse just seems to come together and the four corners are complementing each other, instead of each corner operating as an individual.

At first, this filly wasn't really looking for anywhere to go. Later she was asking, "Well, what do we do?" It's right then—or just before that—when you already know where they are going.

One other fellow in Elko that fall was thinking about timing and working at it. He wasn't having too bad a result. His horse's front end wasn't too bad, but the hind feet weren't in time right. I asked the fellow to go ahead and elevate the front end, and slow the front end a little. When the horse gets in the lope you can check him a little when he is raising, elevating. You help him elevate and just slow his front a little. It will help if you can get the horse to slow his stride in there and he elevates in front. Pretty soon the horse is liable to start reaching under behind for a natural lope. At the beginning this horse was a little bit scattered. (The horse may feel a little hurried and a little tense so he can't really be himself.)

After a bit, as far as I was concerned, things looked all right for this rider. It looked like he would get it. (There were enough times when the horse hit maybe only one stride that was closer, but the fact that it hit once showed the rider that it could be.) So, it will be just trying to get the horse so he will hit that more often. After a while, the horse will hit it maybe two or three times in a row—then he might miss six—next trip around he might miss entirely again. Pretty soon he will be hitting and staying on there more than he is missing. Pretty soon it will be just like breathing for the rider and horse. He won't have to struggle with it.

The thing that I feel is the most important for people to try to recognize and realize is how important it is to keep track of the horse and find out where that horse is all the time. This is what I asked of the people who were watching one morning in Carmel Valley, while Susie was working with her Arabian stallion. This horse had been doing pretty well for Susie at home, until one day as she went to get on, something didn't work out right. The horse got scared and started to leave. Susie was just a little quicker than that and she got up on the side of the saddle and stayed around there until she got the horse stopped. Ever since then, the horse had a troubled spot when Susie started to get on him.

I asked Susie to just pretend she was going to get on. The horse was preparing to move forward, and Susie stopped everything. Then I asked her to get ahold of the saddle horn and put a little weight on it and act like she was going to get on; then to put a little more weight in the stirrup, to feel the horse. The horse looked as if he was going to stay there forever and then he got a little teetery—now that is the body language you look for. Before he even moved, the horse was liable to do what he did. The sooner you can read that or understand it, the better chance the horse has of staying put.

The next time, the horse was a little earlier wanting to move. We watched real close—all this time she was letting him know that she was wanting him to stand.

I told her when it was time to reach for the saddle horn again—there was a time. It's like slapping a person when he's asleep. At that time he isn't going to do anything about it until he wakes up. He is helpless; he can't do anything at that time. When the time is right, the rider can get on the horse and he can't help but stay there, and the rider won't have to abuse him.

In Susie's preparation to get on, there were times when it was right to get on; in the next instant that time had gone by and it wasn't fitting. This was one of the things I was trying to bring out loud and clear, the importance of this preparation.

Soon, it was lasting quite a while. She would wiggle the saddle and prepare; if he moved she would settle him in his tracks. He learned to wait for her—be with her—not try to leave when any little thing happened. At first he thought when the saddle moved he needed to move; he had to get that separated.

In the beginning, the horse was chewing the bit. He was bothered inside and *he was sucking his thumb*, I call it. Then, later, there was a time when everything was right; it was OK to step on.

Another interesting filly we worked with in Carmel Valley was one I described to her rider as a combination horse, dressage horse and trick horse. I told the rider I thought both of them were amazing. You will notice I didn't say what they were *doing* was amazing; but they were something amazing. The filly could pull her little kicking-up act, and the rider didn't fall apart. She would go along with the horse, and pretty soon the horse would go along with her and do real nicely, until the filly decided she wanted to do something again. Now that wasn't all bad. There was an awful lot of good going on there. But this kicking gave me an opportunity to work with the rider and the horse on that. If the rider can put the weight on the foot the horse is thinking of kicking with, it will stay on the ground, and the horse can't kick with it. Then, when the horse starts to move from that, the rider will have the horse going forward, so the horse will have something else to do or think about. The horse forgets about that corner, whichever it might be.

Now that is asking quite a lot of anybody—what I just said—but it can be done, and this rider could do it. The filly's whole leverage was in her back quarters. From the saddle back is where she had that leverage. The filly would draw the line and say, "Now, Martha, I'm going to tell you something; there is a line here and don't you cross it, or I'll kick up or something."

Then the rider would need to say, "Now, filly, there's a line out here, and you are going to cross it."

And the filly would go across it.

Now the thing is, on one like this, when they are trying to take over and take advantage of you, you kind of go along with their game, but you let them hang themselves—beat themselves at their own game, more or less.

This filly could be responsive and right on one instant, and then the next instant she would shut everything off. "When she was good, she was very, very good, and when she was bad, she was horrid."

I had Martha just start off doing something the filly didn't seem to want to do. Then at the time when I could see an opportunity to work in variety (and a variation of this variety), to keep the filly working so that she didn't have any place to go to get ahold, I would suggest these things to the rider.

I felt this was really good for all the group to see.

I would have Martha back her, then change directions before the filly could take over. Then go forward before the horse could get set in there—then changed directions. If the filly started to kick up, I would have Martha raise up on a rein that would cause the horse's body weight to be off balance so the filly couldn't get in position to get her hind feet off the ground. Martha would keep her from getting braced on a corner. She couldn't get her head down. She couldn't get her feet up. You see, if Martha headed into some of these things when the filly started to put on her little act, pretty soon all Martha would have to do was say, "Now settle down!" and this filly was smart enough to do it. If you can keep the horse moving, keep him from getting his head down and his feet up, and keep him from bracing on you, *he has to go.* This filly couldn't do anything but go forward. She might kick up for a while, but then Martha would catch her on the corner, and set those hind feet right down.

It was really great for all to watch as long as Martha was doing all the work. But there was a point when Martha said she felt she couldn't quite do it fast enough.

I told her it was beautiful. She was beginning to get caught up with the filly to where she could head her off. With this type of horse the rider wouldn't want to confine her too much; she could get to kicking up more or rearing up. She needed to keep her going, keep her on the corners, to keep the horse from getting the head straight down and pulling the rider off. She needed to keep it open so the horse could go. (You wouldn't want to confine one like that in just a small area.)

This wasn't an easy horse, but already Martha was catching up. More and more she had the time she needed to fix it so that the filly got herself in trouble when she tried something. Martha was presenting that to the filly more often than in the beginning, and she was riding her on through. Yet she was not keeping her too confined. At this stage of the game it is most important to be able to go somewhere. I would say that is where many people would lose a horse like this. They would try to confine the horse too much.

Up on the far end of the ring, the filly wanted to kick up, and every time Martha had her someplace else. The filly tried all kinds of places, but *Martha was there*, and Martha just rode her on through. Martha would open up there, take the pressure off and ride her on through.

Martha was doing great, and I asked the group to notice how nicely the filly's tail was hanging.

Martha had confidence in herself then, because she knew she was going to have time to gather the filly up before it was too late. She could tell when the resistance was leaving and she could open up, gradual-like.

A rider needs to always do all he possibly can to help the horse. With another group of riders, once, we were working with a horse on picking up a hind foot problem. Actually, this horse had two problems. She didn't want to stand still; she wanted to move. She had to learn how to stand and stay put. The other problem was that she had to learn to stand on three feet. She kept moving, just about the time that she could maybe balance and stand there. She would get the idea of moving, so that spoiled the chance of her getting balanced.

Here is what a person could do there: if you will pick that foot up again and use the toe, it will help the horse to balance. You can tip their weight so you can help them learn to stand there.

Pick up the hind foot, ahold of the toe—now you can bend the ankle—keep the hock bent, get your other hand on the hip bone, so that if the horse starts to move he doesn't pull away.

Once you get to working this, it is pretty easy just to slip your hand down the leg, and the foot winds up in the palm of your hand, and with your other hand on the hip, you can draw up. The horse doesn't seem to get the leverage on you.

You don't have to get that toe; if you are not used to doing it that way you may try to grab for it, and that may disturb the horse. I want to mention there is a caution there.

In recognizing a relaxed horse it can be as plain as if things were written in big letters on the side of the barn, how it operates within the horse. It's just as plain as it can be—*it's real*. But, people can look at a horse and not *actually see what's taking place*. It is the person's responsibility to see that horse, to see where the person can help the horse on different things. A person needs to start trying to analyze, or understand the horse, where he can help the horse on things he is going to ask him to do, or even not do.

The approach a person takes is *very important*—the way a person approaches, with understanding. When you start to approach is when you either get the resistance or the receptive response. That is where you really help the horse to start out. This is where it can really break down when people don't follow through. They may not even realize there is this part of the horse they need to understand or figure out. They may be trying to go at the horse in a way that says, "Here is something I want you to do. You get busy and do it, or else."

You have to arrange it so the horse is first—his naturalness, his self-preservation. You arrange it so it is easy to do the things you are asking the horse to do. If he is trying to do the wrong thing, you arrange it so that is difficult. Anytime the horse heads in the direction you are asking, it is wide open. There is no resistance, so the horse learns to experience this.

Last fall I was helping a girl who had a nice black horse. The horse had been raced. She got the horse because he wasn't going to do well enough as a race horse, but he was a good moving horse. She got him for a calf-roping horse and for barrel racing. He is a nice horse but he has been real tight. This girl is making progress with the horse, quite a bit of progress. For a while when he started into a lope he was so tight he wanted to crow hop. I mentioned that the best thing I know for this is trotting—a lot of trotting. Start out slow and bring it up to an extended trot. If it starts to get tight or bothered, slow down and then come up again until he can get on a tetter from a trot to a lope. When I saw the black horse a couple of weeks later, the girl had him really trotting good. The horse was a little tight yet, but not bad; he was staying with her. He wasn't getting lost and breaking his speed.

Later when this girl was trying to get this black horse so she could swing her rope on him, she would start to swing her arm, and he got real bothered. I watched a little while, then I said, "When you start to swing your arm, first, just maybe, pet him a little on the neck, on the rump, then swing your arm, not a full swing; maybe hold your arm closer to you."

When she started, she had possibly overdone it, more than what he could take at that time. (She is a good kid. She does real well.) Then, when she would swing, she could touch him if she didn't come too far. I told her if she felt him getting bothered to withdraw, then come back.

Pretty soon she could get closer and closer when the horse started to come out of it, which was pretty quick. I told her to take her left hand and see what he did there. It didn't bother him at all on the left side. It made me feel maybe that the jockey had been right handed with his whip. Pretty soon that horse wouldn't have any problem at all on either side when he found out he wasn't going to get hurt. If people could just have an understanding of what is causing the horse's problem.

One of the fellows in his feedback did a good job of explaining a smiliar situation. Had this girl read that, maybe she could have related it to her horse and got this working; but again, she could have read that and missed it. But the fellow did a good job of explaining how it had worked for him—how valuable it had been for a lot of things. You can just go right on; it can be all shaping up. You can be taking care of things before they happen, a lot of times. A rider can channel things in a proper direction far ahead, before it ever gets to where it is going to surface, and there will be other things that can be building toward it. This is so difficult to put into wiritng. People can see it happen when I am helping with a problem, and that is an experience in itself, and it helps up to a point. But it is hard for people to visualize, experience or recognize all that is taking place or even a part of it. It has been a problem for me to try to present these things to people so that they understand them well enough. It has to be understood, and then a person has to learn how to apply it. It's like if you start to do something with one hand or the other. You've already been writing with your right hand and you start to write with your left hand. You know what you want to write, but your coordination will hold you back. I don't know just how to get it into writing so it will draw people's attention strongly enough to get their interest, to the point that if it were there in print they would stay with it long enough to be able to separate things and get it. It is so ever-varying, what you are doing, depending on one horse or the other.

Once when I was helping a group, there was a two-year-old filly that had been ridden some before, and she was pretty switchy. The fellow asked me if I had ever done anything about a horse's switchy tail.

"No!" I said. Seems like if you can find out what is causing the irritation that is causing the tail to move, you can help overcome that problem and *the tail will take care of itself.* Just forget about the tail and try to figure out what is causing the problem, then work from there. I told the fellow, "Just forget about the tail. Don't try to keep the tail from switching."

I don't know what that rider got done. The tail is just an indication of an irritation somewhere else that is causing the tail to move. This so often happens with the horse. People will recognize the symptom but not the real cause of the problem. Sometimes when I go to help people who say they are having a problem with a horse, I tell the person I am the horse's lawyer and the horse is having a "people problem."

There are so many things to bring out, you can't corner them all in a book, but they are so important. Sometimes a person can work *around* a lot of spots without working *through* them. A person has to get things separated. That may take a little while to get operating. It depends on the approach, how to get it to fit in and operate.

With one group of riders a few years ago, two riders were especially concerned about their horses' backing. It was good to have the two to compare. The gelding was lively enough on his feet and his knees bent real well, while the mare had trouble bending her knees. The gelding acted like he was not too sure that he should put his foot back. He wasn't too bad a horse to use to demonstrate a little about the time to draw on the rein to help him move his foot. He was just picking up his foot mostly. He was moving it a little but he was not really reaching. When the foot is leaving the ground and starting up, the rider needs to encourage it to come on back. When a horse is taking care of that pretty well, it doesn't take much, but this horse was unsure just what to do with his feet, so he needed to have some help to encourage him to reach. It was just a matter of the horse knowing what to do with himself. He needed the rider to direct and support him more. Pretty soon he got more confidence.

When the mare was asked to move back, her head would go up and her feet would stick. She didn't seem to know what to do; she would hang there. I suggested the rider let the mare get in there and then try to keep her hunting to get out. After a while, the horse won't try to get in that spot. If the horse starts in, give the horse the chance to come out of those hunting-up spots, and if she doesn't, just let her get in deeper until she can work her way out. That's a case of letting the wrong things become difficult and the right things easy. Soon the mare's feet were starting to move. I had the rider firm up and draw and bring her on through. The mare was starting to be able to separate things a little. Then she sort of hung up again. Then she got with it and her feet were moving back.

When I am working with a person and his horse, I can help him get in a position so the horse can find the response we are working for. Trying to put this into words so a reader can get a picture of what is taking place is not easy for me. Some of the terminology may cause a problem, like the rider who didn't have much idea what was meant by the expression, "the horse's feet are stuck." There are a lot of things that way, it seems. The expression "hunting-up spot" is sometimes a new expression to a rider, but as we work on things together the rider begins to recognize this stage in the horse's learning process. The rider needs to experience this as well as the horse.

In Nevada one fall a fellow was riding a colt. The weather warmed up, and this fellow decided to shed his coat. This caused the colt to want to shed the rider. The fellow wasn't very bothered so I told him he could use the horse's little bothered spot to get the horse used to moving with him. He just took the colt in a circle, and when the colt let down you could see the horse soften. The horse got so the curve of his body was fitting the curve the person was traveling. It wasn't bent one way while the rider was traveling the other way.

The rider could feel the horse soften. The horse felt good to the rider and lightened up on the head. His feet were alive and they were responsive. It almost looked like the rider had the horse's feet in his hands.

Some days when there are little bothered spots in the horse, a person can just put that to work for them. You don't have to take it all out, all at once. The horse will learn a lot of getting with the rider just by the little bit this horse and rider went through. The horse was hunting for the rider instead of trying to get out and leave the whole thing. He wanted to get close to the rider instead of just getting away from the coat.

Another time with a group of riders, mostly riding colts, one fellow mentioned that green horses seem to have a tendency to drift toward a bunch of horses. He said that was a problem he had riding colts at home through a pasture. He was asking about some of the things he could do to help the horse stay with him and on course without getting in there and hanging up. So, we worked a little on that. We used the group of riders there as if they were released horses in a pasture. It wasn't quite the same as being home at the ranch, but I felt it might help the rider get an idea, and then when he got home he could experiment a little bit with it. But I cautioned him if it didn't seem quite right to just forget about what I had said; his self-preservation should come first. Sometimes people might try to do what they thought I said, and the situation might not be just right for it. I told him, "If it doesn't seem right just forget about me—right at that time—take a fresh start some other day, or maybe the same day."

I've had people so serious about trying to do things just exactly right, and I wasn't around there to stop them, and they would get themselves in a spot that was a little bit dangerous. That is why I say, "Do what seems to be best to do for yourself." Somebody might take a different approach to some of the things I say and get the same effect. They might get the same results, and sometimes better, than what I would have gotten.

I don't think of it as trying to do it exact or the same, because there *is* that difference in individuals. Just think of *you* as doing it and don't try to think, "This is what Tom would do." Try to leave enough in where it seems to fit what we have been working for. You may just change a little bit and it will seem to fit better. You need to follow your own feelings on that. I told this rider a little of how I worked with something similar at home, and we worked a little around the bunch of horses that was there. I wanted to get something going for him so when he got home he could handle it, even though it would be a very different situation at home.

At home when I'm on a pretty green horse, I approach the loose horses in the pasture so that when they start to move they'll be going in the direction that I want them to go. After they start I'll be going another direction, and when they get out of sight, or at a far enough distance, then I'll bend my horse back to where he will come on later. If I were trying to follow too close he'd want to get up with them. You keep your horse occupied and pretty soon he doesn't know where those other horses are; he gets with you, and then it won't matter. When your horse gets with you, the other horses aren't the main attraction. You can ride around them and right through the bunch and out the other side.

Sometimes if you are starting some colts and have the loose horses out in the pasture, if you just circle those horses they will get so they will collect in a small area. They will stand there, and you can ride around them one way and the other, and then you can ride right through the middle of the bunch and out the other side. If they start to scatter, you just circle them, and they will huddle in there. You don't have to have a fence in sight for that to work, and the horse you are riding gets used to going where you point him. We worked on that some so the fellow could get an idea of the approach he would take when he got home. It was not so important what he got worked out that day; it was done so he would be exposed to things to work on. When he got home he could do some experimenting then. I told him not to try too hard to make it work to start with; just to give it time for things to shape up.

Sometimes if there is a hill in the pasture, I'll lope my horse up that hill and then come around, and if the horse didn't feel just right, I'd work my way down and come up again. Take a little of the air out of them and then get around where the bunch of horses is and start the horses and then go a different direction—don't try to stay too close to the horses. Then when you come in, the horse is sort of disconnected from the loose ones. It's just surprising how quickly it doesn't matter where you are or what horse you are on: they have life and all—but they are with you.

When you are riding around a group of horses, especially in an arena, you need to be aware of the other horses' attitudes as well as your own. The horses will tell you if you are listening to them. It may seem to the rider that a horse will all of a sudden kick out at another horse. But had the rider been more aware, he could have felt this shaping up in his horse, or the attitude of the horse that started the disturbance.

A roan gelding and a sorrell gelding demonstrated this very problem for a group of riders one day in Carmel Valley. No one was hurt, but it was a good learning experience for everyone. As the roan horse and his rider were coming around the arena, that sorrel horse told the roan horse not to come any closer, quite a ways back. The roan horse saw, but the rider didn't, and the rider didn't yield any. All the rider would have had to do was to just move over—probably an inch would have done it—two feet would have been more than ample. But the rider kept going. The sorrel horse kept saying, "No! I draw the line!" The roan horse was going to stay there with the rider against his own need for self-preservation, but when the sorrell really began to say, "I mean it," the roan horse moved over, even though he was trying his best to stay with his rider.

These are things that are so important for a person to recognize. I believe they speak of that as body language. Maybe that's a good term. It was very loud and clear. It may have looked just like two horses were meeting, but there was a lot more going on besides just meeting.

All this was a help to all the people there, no matter whether they had an English saddle or a Western saddle. These riders were all good riders who could do just about anything they would like to do, if they understood the horse better.

The rider of the roan horse has a terrific amount of feel and tremendous timing. He is agile and his reflexes are good. I'm sure horses like him. I know the rest of us do. It's just a matter of listening to the horse, and the horse will tell him more than I can. *All I am is the horse's lawyer.* I might mention, when I was very young a mule told me about some of these things. That mule told me way in advance not to get any closer, but I thought I knew more than that mule, and I limped for two weeks.

So, you might say I learned about this the hard way, but I was young enough that I have gotten good use of that sore leg for over sixty-five years.

It seems like it is a little hard for riders even to think about trying to do something when everything seems to be going along all right. They don't realize that is the time to get the horse to feeling with them a little so that by the time they get to this other spot the horse is already occupied, or they have it so they can carry on through. That's a real difficult spot, it seems, to try to help someone realize the importance of having this prearranged before he ever gets to the spot where there is going to be a problem. That's one spot I'd like to try to elaborate on so that it is clear for the reader. When a person is right there with his horse, and I am there talking about it, and it isn't too easy to understand it or get it to operating, it will be even more difficult to get it into a book. On the other hand, if the person could get a picture of it in reading, it might be easier to visualize. Then when they got on their own, they might be able to figure it out and get it to operating. Some people may be able to get it better that way than if I were there trying to explain or to say when.

Like getting those back quarters. Say the horse is operating strong to the left. The back quarters are liable to be over to the right, and the head and neck are a little past center to the left. If the rider tries to take ahold of the right hand rein, the neck will overbend and will get a sag in, so that the shoulder is going out to the right a little. Until the back quarters shape up, you are pretty helpless on the front end. Instead of letting that horse drift and get the timing to try to help let go and reach behind, the rider will be pulling on the front end, and that puts more sag in the front and more brace in the rear. In order to try to break that brace in the rear quarters, there is a time when you draw and lift so that it gets the rear quarters to yield. When those feet are on the ground, you are not going to move them. It's when they are leaving the ground, before they get to the peak and start down, you direct that. A person's timing needs to be right on. Failure comes when the rider's timing is just opposite, or the horse is positioned just opposite to what is needed.

I was watching a boy on a lively filly. The boy was a good boy, pretty agile and rode well. The filly was smart with a lot of go. Whenever the filly wanted to go, they would just go. She was one-sided and any time she wanted to cut out on him, like going around the arena, if she didn't want to come on around the bend, she cut out to the left. The filly would get braced behind and get her neck and head and front set, so that when she wanted to go on out she'd just go. The rider was doing just the same each time as he had done the time before. She had made a little progress, but the rider could have arranged it so that the filly was with him and handling before he got to that area where she was liable to cut out. The way it was, by the time she decided to cut out, *she went.* She might go on around one time, or two or three times, and then she'd sell out on him again. He wasn't riding any different whether she did or didn't and it had already happened and was a little late to try to make a recovery. If this young rider had realized the importance of having things arranged before he came to this problem spot, he probably wouldn't have been having a problem.

A few months ago I was helping a young man with his horse. This was a horse that was real scared inside. It was terrible that the horse got in that situation. Finally he began to realize what we were offering him was real, that it could be. *There is a big responsibility to not destroy that.* I told the group that horse needed lots and lots of petting. He has found out for the first time in his life he doesn't have to be scared.

Usually when a horse begins to understand this, he takes the better way. But that's a real delicate situation. If the person doesn't understand it, when the horse is starting to find it, he can destroy what he's been trying to help the horse do. So many times people do that!

So many riders are more or less struggling, trying to analyze the situation, trying to get the picture of what is really happening, trying to figure out the approach that might correct it in a useful way. I wish I knew how to put words together so it would just clear up a lot of these things.

When I am helping an individual with his horse, I find we are only able to do what that horse and rider are ready for. Working with a group of riders, sometimes things work out where one rider and horse will be able to come through on a learning situation in such a way that the rest of the group gets a pretty good picture of what the meaning was. But when those riders go to physically apply it themselves, it may be a different picture. They may just not be ready. It's like if you are used to doing something with your right hand, it's hard to do it with your left hand, even if you know exactly what you want to do. Your reflexes don't just do it the first time. That's the way it is many times with the horse. Often people don't allow that consideration for the horse; they think the horse ought to do it the first time he is asked. The rider couldn't even do any different, if he were being asked, but he thinks the horse ought to do it.

One rider and his horse able to make a good picture for all of us one day was Joe. The day before I had visited with Joe about the importance of straightness in a horse and the problem of a horse getting one sided. We had talked about using an imaginary line to follow, and he had worked on that some. On this morning, when Joe rode into the ring, I asked him to notice that his horse's head was a little to the left. It was not hanging straight with his body. I asked him to come on forward *right straight*, and just go with the horse. When he did, those ears held steady and the horse's head hung right straight down the middle.

Then again, I told Joe to let the horse come right on, there was a spot there to let the horse come right on through, just *right straight on*. Otherwise his head would get to hanging just a little off center. But Joe opened it up so the horse had something he knew he could do and he was interested in. The horse's ears stayed just right. Then when Joe needed to bend a little the horse was right on that line that I spoke about earlier. The rider will have the line picked before he gets there, and it will work just like this did for Joe. When you are working on this, sometimes the horse will have it picked and the rider will go along with this; *that's fine*. You accompany the horse first, then you get him to accompany you; then you accompany each other. That is the unity. You are one. Whenever you go, you are one. When the horse's ears go forward, if the rider isn't ready to go right with those ears, there will likely be a little hesitation before he goes. Then when the horse does go the ears may not be forward. These are things a rider will get worked out. Then, each step you can, increase the speed.

I told Joe what he was doing looked good. His horse's head was a little to one side but not bad. All through his body everything was going, and when Joe asked the horse to settle down a little slower, the horse was right with him, and then he was ready to go on out again. It's like a swing. It swings out and swings back. Joe was helping the horse take care of the corners as he came around the ring. He was already thinking about the second corner before he ever turned toward it. There were times when those feet were missing, but Joe could feel that. He helped the horse settle down, and those feet became sure. On those corners, as the horse was coming into them, Joe was trying to help the horse think about the other side of the corner and round it out. Before the horse got one side finished Joe was letting him know about this other one, and before he even got into it, when he felt the horse was going to handle that, Joe was letting the horse know where they were going to be going next.

I asked Joe to let his horse know way early. I told him, "He's the type of a person, *that horse is*, that likes to know before he goes to bed tonight what the next day is going to be; instead of waiting until after breakfast and then starting to think about it. That horse is a way early. If he doesn't know way early, it bothers him. He may not sleep."

Going into the next corner I asked Joe to ease off on him and let the horse find his way out, and the same with the following corner. When the horse felt like he was going to make it, the rider was to ease off. Let the horse do as much as he possibly can without getting lost.

It is the same way when the rider starts to leave the border and come off; just let the horse know, give him a little room and see how little it takes. Then before you get out too far let the horse know you are going to go back up the other way.

For a while Joe was trying to do more than was needed on that horse. It took very little, so Joe eased off. All this horse needed by this time was to get the message of where the rider wanted to go. Joe left it to the horse to see how much the horse could handle for himself. If the horse needed a little support, a little directing, Joe would try to help him at the time he needed it. Joe was finally able to put the reins down on the saddle. The horse was ready to take care of it.

I told Joe the horse almost didn't need him—but I emphasized I'd said *almost*.

It made a good picture for all the group. Not every horse or every rider there was ready to do this, but it was good to see what can be.

Whenever I work with riders I keep trying to help them get the picture of straightness in a horse. This is so important because this is the way the horse wants to travel and be *relaxed*. Over the years I have worked with different people over this straightness or lack of straightness in a horse. When horses are not traveling straight, they will make the transition but they will not be positioned correctly, so they can't be quite as effective. It can't be quite as comfortable for the horse, or the rider, or to look at. It doesn't look as good as if they positioned for whatever move they were going to make.

I'm not right sure whether the horses get to the left first from getting more exercise toward the left than the right. The person goes to catch them from the left, puts the halter on from the left, puts the saddle on from the left, generally. After they have gotten on from the left they nearly always turn to the left, unless there is a real need to go to the right. Then if the rider starts to get straight, the horse is liable to turn its head and neck toward the left before its feet start going straight ahead.

I don't know if the person just gets to accepting the horse being in that position or whether the person is operating that way himself and causing the horse to get to the left.

I'm pretty sure once the rider gets the horse to operating that way, traveling crooked if the horse is straight (one they haven't been riding), that horse doesn't feel good to the rider. He is liable to start riding him so he is *crooked*. I'm pretty sure that will happen if he is not thinking about it. If he is thinking about it, he is liable to have it taken care of. I have ridden horses people had been riding that were crooked. I had watched these people ride, and they were riding the horse that way. Maybe, after I had ridden the horse, the horse would start to go straight, but then if that same person started riding the horse again, he would go crooked again. I'm sure it is a whole lot in the operation of the person, and it isn't real easy for the person to overcome. I've visited with different ones about this over the years. I've asked them which shoe they put on first, which arm they put down the coat sleeve first, or which foot they shoved down their pants leg first. If they checked themselves on that, they were liable to find they were always using the same side.

As the rider learns to be more aware of where the horse is, he will be able to pinpoint more where he needs the help. As he understands more of the horse, then the rider will start to help the horse where he needs the help, and it will make it easier for everyone.

I remember several years ago Ray Hunt and I were visiting one evening about a problem with a horse. One person listening said, "That would be a case of the sickness being somewhere besides where the symptoms indicated."

That can happen. You can make a mistake in interpreting where the sickness is. You need to get that taken care of so the rest will all shape up in place.

Lynette explained her problem as the horse getting the left shoulder out. To her it seemed that this was where the sickness was, *in the shoulder*, and that was where she was working.

We visited about that. I asked if she felt the shoulder was wanting to kind of bulge instead of rounding out. It seemed to me the horse might feel like he had swallowed a broomstick on that side. There was not much flex right in the middle along the ribs under the rider's thigh.

I asked Lynette to think about the rear quarter on the left. I told her I was going to make a guess that when she was coming toward the left, if she could get the rear left quarter to get more over, instead of swinging into the inside, if it would loosen up, be a little free-er over as the horse was making those curves, then the horse's backbone would fit the contour of the course that they were going, his head would be hanging straight with the rest of him to fit that contour—and *then the shoulder would be taken care of.* The sickness was in the back corner, and when that was taken care of, the rest of it all shaped up in place. When we were working to find the problem, everyone in the group had heard the symptom. Then we had Lynette ride out and do the good side first. We all watched what was going on. Then Lynette turned, and we watched to see if that other side didn't do quite as well. We tried to see what was happening different, so that the sides weren't the same. The performance wasn't coming out quite as nice on one side as it was on the other. We compared the two, and that gave us a chance to try to help the horse do better on the side that was not so good, without taking away any of the good part of the good side.

Lynette was asked where it felt like the horse needed help. She was comparing the two sides to see if there was any place in there that felt enough different so she could recognize where the horse needed help the most. Many of the group felt like they could see that the left side of the horse was stiffer; most of them felt he needed a lot of help on the left shoulder. It takes time and experience to learn to diagnose a sickness and prescribe a treatment, even when a person can recognize the symptoms.

The next rider that day was having a little problem as he was going to the left. The right shoulder wanted to push out. His back quarters did not seem too bad to the rider, but he definitely noticed the problem in the horse's head and neck and his shoulder. I told him if he got the hind quarters moving good, the front part wouldn't be trouble. One of the things that might help with a problem like this is to use the right hand rein to draw back and up so it will shorten the front corner. That one you will use to draw this corner in and open up on the other side. It will be in time with the horse's feet, and that is likely to help him. Pretty soon, as this starts to work, you will be listening to that back corner. What you are doing there actually is taking care of that. You will be feeling of the back part, and you won't have to be thinking so much of what is going on in front.

I asked the rider if he wanted to experiment a little. I asked him to canter straight up the border and feel for how straight he was going. If he was going to the left, to feel whether his back end was over to the left a little. Even though this horse was pretty green yet, to expect him to canter straight. Then the rider did the same thing to the right of the ring. Some horses have a tendency to want to get their front feet over toward the border and their back end out a little. So what the rider will do is keep the front feet out a little and try to keep the back end from moving too far away from the border. This is something the rider can do that I believe will help the horse. A little of that exercise might help. I told the rider to do a little of that and then go back in the circle one way and the other. When he started again, I asked the rider to think about the horse's feet, to think about not leaving until the horse's feet were ready to go. The horse will soon get so when you pick up the reins his feet will start to get ready and then they will move *right on*. Then I had the rider make some bends one way, then the other. The horse was feeling a little better to the rider than he had been, but he was not feeling quite what the rider would like. I suggested the rider give the horse just a little more time as he was shaping up, to start to feel into those. I asked him to give the horse just a little more time and not bend the horse quite so much, to see if the horse would find a place for his back end.

When you feel the horse start to come through don't confine him in the front, just open up there and let him straighten out on his own—with maybe just a little support and direction—*but very little*. Then when he gets straight and is still moving forward, change directions. Don't try to get it too early. When the horse lets go, give him room. What that will do is keep the drive for him. Pretty soon all you have to do is reach and he will shape right up without putting an extra bend in.

Soon, the horse was responding pretty well for the rider; he was preparing when the rider just let him know. The horse was filling in, and that is what I like to see. I had the rider give the horse a little extra room, as the horse was getting to where he was keeping that shoulder pushed out a little, his neck and head were bent around a little too much, and he wasn't coming on through behind. This way it let him complete the swing behind. The horse wasn't calloused in any way and all he needed was to learn how. Soon, he wouldn't know any difference. A horse has to learn, just like a person.

The next horse we worked with that day loped a little long; he was kind of all on the ground. I thought he was to a point where the rider could maybe start helping him elevate a little more. This would slow the time that the horse started down, and give his back end a little more time to catch up in those strides. As the horse is coming up he gets to the peak, and he'll ease off.

Then, when the horse was going along the border he was wanting to travel with his front feet close to the border and his back ones out a little, even in the walk or trot. I asked the rider to work a little on that, to keep seeing how little it takes to keep the horse from getting too much toward the border. I told the rider not to try to get it all at once. If the horse swings in toward the border occasionally, even if he bumps it a little, that isn't too bad at this stage. You need to ease off just every bit you can when he is not too close to the border. Then, if he gets too close to the border, even if he bumps himself on it, don't worry; pretty soon he will watch where his front and back feet are. Pretty soon you won't have to do quite as much; the horse will take care of the straightness himself. At first you may try to help the horse a little too much and keep him from finding it. It looks good when you don't have to push the horse at any time, but just give the horse a little support and a little directing. The horse will begin to come down there with his ears forward. This looks good, and I'm sure it feels good to the horse.

This rider was looking better all the time. When he was out there pointing his horse somewhere, he would point him and then he would wait to see if the horse was going to look where the rider was thinking. The rider was trying to let the horse know where he was looking and where he was wanting to go. I told this rider he could maybe draw him, point him and then see where he went; that maybe the horse would go there, and maybe he wouldn't, but to give him the opportunity. If you keep the horse too confined it is liable to be in the way of him looking for a place to go. You might have to hang there too long. The horse can be to a place where the rider doesn't have to be all that close to him all the time. It is the same way out on those bends. You can maybe just ask the horse, nip him just a little, then ease off to see where he is going. And then if he needs another nip, see how little you can do. Don't try to get it all the first time. Pretty soon if he feels you reach, he won't come against the pressure. For a while you will have to nip it, once for sure, maybe twice, maybe three times. Then pretty soon he will feel you reach, and there he will come. If you keep too close too long, that interferes with his getting this flexibility all through his body. The horse will find it, and soon you'll start to reach and he'll know the meaning. You try to use less and less for him to get to doing more and more.

Emphasizing Some Vital Concepts

Corral Fence Gumption

It may seem like you will never get anything accomplished, but sometimes going slow is the quickest way to get there.

o   o   o

At first the horse needs to start to understand that there is a little meaning there. He won't see the purpose yet, but later he will begin to see the purpose. Then, when you go to reach for him, he knows what to do. He is planning ahead.   The horse can be exploring all kinds of avenues of escape, but not have it figured out that the relief is right out through the feet.

o   o   o

It won't be very long until when the rider reaches for the horse, the horse will start to prepare to position and the feet will move just like the rider had the feet in his fingers.

o   o   o

I like to see the horse be with the rider and know what he is asking him to do, but still take in the surroundings, too. If you feel the horse starting to anticipate, change directions before he gets over-exposed.

o   o   o

You feel and listen to the horse. The experience of the results of his response helps you understand for the next time.

o   o   o

If they get their heads and necks too low when they are backing, they get long on the ground and low in the back.

o   o   o

When it starts getting effective for you, it is easier to get your timing.

Until those feet move where you need them, the horse is going to be where he is.

o   o   o

You will try to get the results in various different approaches, so you don't wear any one of them out.

o   o   o

It may seem at first that pressure is something the horse is wanting, but the last thing he would like to be doing is *putting pressure on himself*, but he doesn't know what else to do. It is our responsibility to help him overcome his problem.

o   o   o

We are trying to build up the horse's confidence. We're trying to get him brave in his feet. His feet are really scared so we are trying to get his feet to be brave.

o   o   o

The horse is learning to yield to that firmness. We are trying to present it to him as if he puts that pressure on himself, and when he figures out it's him that's putting the pressure on, then he finds a way to relieve himself of that pressure by yielding to his own pressure. *Then it beomes his idea.*

o   o   o

The horse needs to get it separated and get the message to his feet.

o   o   o

Sometimes a horse needs a little more support, a little more direction to follow through, like a wheelbarrow coming up against a high spot needing just a little more help to get it over.

o   o   o

Sometimes a horse would like to do the training; he gets to calling the shots.

o   o   o

Riders need to realize sometimes that horses need soothing, cuddling and comforting. Sometimes that isn't too bad for people either. They can use that a little bit, too.

o   o   o

So many times even when people are working for straightness in a horse, they may think the horse is straight and it isn't.

o   o   o

Try to take the uncertainty out of it for the horse; let him get more secure.

Sometimes when a horse has had quite a little work and kind of gets up a sweat—I like to just stay on him and while he is cooling out—drying off—just let him kind of be there to explore a little. It's so much better than if you just unsaddle him hot. I really like to do that if I have a chance.

o   o   o

The rider can be trying to help the horse too much. If you were out having to do a job, that help would be all right, but if you are helping your horse to learn to do something, he won't have a chance unless you fix it for him to learn.

o   o   o

When the horse gets to yielding through the back quarters, the front end will be easy.

o   o   o

I was not trying to keep the horse from getting into things. I let him get in there and then tried to keep him hunting to get out. If he started in, I would give him the chance to come out of those hunting up spots, and if he didn't, I'd just let him get in deeper until he could work his way out. That would be a case of letting the wrong things become difficult and the right things easy.

o   o   o

If the horse is wanting to throw a sag and get dull on his feet, you get those two sides loosened up and his feet will come right on through.

o   o   o

A person has a tendency to try to straighten that out too quick, and the horse gets a sag in them and their feet slow down, or else they kind of curl under like a snail on the corners.

o   o   o

Earlier there wasn't any use to allow leeway for the horse to find it because he would have only gone into it or he wouldn't have done anything; now, the less interference you can do, the better control you'll get. You don't have to have a lot of slack there especially, but the horse will operate just like your fingers. The control of those feet and legs and throughout his body. The horse has to learn and that takes time.

o   o   o

Once the horse gets to responding, then you try to get the response you are asking for with less. You try to cut down what you are applying and get more response with less pressure, until it almost gets to be just a thought.

o   o   o

You think, and that horse feels something going on in your body and he is ready to go. It may not be that way for quite a while and it may never get to be, but that is what you have in mind.

o   o   o

If the horse starts to kind of curl up like a snail on that, don't try to go on into the canter. Come back down to a trot, then bring him up there to where he feels like he will take it. Work him just this side of where he is trying to take over. Just don't let him take over. With some of these other things you'll just let him hang himself. If it gets to where it isn't any fun, then he will be ready to go to work.

o   o   o

There are times you can set it up so that if it is just right, the horse can give it to himself with quite a lot of meaning—so that he will respond to it physically at that time. Then, mentally, he won't forget about what happened to him physically, and mentally he will start thinking about responding. When he does, these little things won't irritate him. His ears will be looking for somewhere to go.

o   o   o

The thing you are trying to help the horse do is to use his own mind. You are trying to present something and then let him figure out how to get there.

o   o   o

You try to make it as easy for the horse as you can. You watch for the opportune time, that is the most fitting time to help the horse learn.

o   o   o

The less directing you have to do the better. Sometimes you have to do quite a bit of directing, other times it's hardly any.

o   o   o

The horse knows where the person is all the time. Now we are trying to help the person know where the horse is all the time. The horse knows where the person is; the person needs to learn to catch up with the horse on that.

o   o   o

Wait for his feet. No matter if you miss your lunch, just hang in there. He is trying to push and get you to yield. He is on his own pressure; you are just fixing it. Don't try to move his feet. *Leave that to him.*

o o o

You are trying to present it in a way that will be the easiest for the horse to understand. You are trying to present it at a time and in a way that will be the easiest for the horse to learn how.

o o o

A person needs to learn to try to get there early—before it happens.

o o o

The horse isn't trying to do the wrong thing. He is trying to do what he thinks he is supposed to do. He is doing it, because it is what *they,* both horse and rider, *have been living.*

o o o

It won't be very long until when you want the horse to slow down or stop, you'll give him the message of whichever it is you want to do, and then you will ease off and he will take care of the rest. I don't mean you will throw him away, but you will just ease off and he will come. *That's the goal.*

o o o

The rider is trying to present it to the horse in such a way that if the horse doesn't yield he is putting pressure on himself. The rider is trying to allow the horse the opportunity to get it separated in order to realize that he is putting pressure on himself, so he will yield to that pressure.

o o o

Don't have the tendency to want to hurry and not let the horse find it. You fix and wait for them to find it; then it's their idea when they move their feet.

o o o

Before you ever start to reach to ask your horse to do something you should have in mind what you are asking and where you are trying to direct.

o o o

I like to see the rider try to work with the naturalness the horse is born with and to *put it to use.*

o o o

The first important thing is to think about riding the horse straight out—between your hands and your legs. Have the life come straight through his body.

At first it seems pretty hard to keep track of the feel and the timing and what the horse's thoughts are. Later on you don't have to think so much about it. It gets like breathing.

o   o   o

In working with people and trying to help them with something, I find it isn't easy for me to try to get them to work in the area where it seems they need to work. They keep trying to work at the end result.

o   o   o

A lot of people get along pretty well with their horses until they go to training those horses.

o   o   o

The horse may not be doing the thing that is the right thing for what the rider is asking him, but as far as the horse is concerned, he is doing the right thing.

Editorial Note: Be Aware

In the last five years a tape recorder has been used as an aide in most of the gathering and harvesting for this project. Until the hours spent on this work it had not occurred to me how much of our day-to-day communication is non-verbal. I have stacks of tapes that contain only a few complete sentences. They do, however, contain a lot of reference material, much of which was used in various ways for this book. In the quiet of Tom's living room, partial sentences would sometimes cover several pages as Tom reconstructed situations and filled in between the lines from the various tapes gathered at the arena.

One beautiful March day, towards the beginning of my taping for the book, I was able to tape a whole working session from beginning to end. Practically the only interruption was when I stopped to change the tape. It was taped in La Grange, California, out beside the corral in a picture postcard setting; all the hills were California-spring-green and covered with flowers. If I had requested a perfect spring day, likely it would not have been so complete as this one.

Tom Butler had come by to visit Tom Dorrance and had brought a young filly he had started a short time before.

Since the visit had been prearranged, a few days earlier, Molly and I had been included; I had my tape recorder, and Molly had questions to ask.

The material in the appendix is this taped session just as it was recorded.

From the first time, years before, I had seen Tom's philosophy in practice, and had realized the difference its application could make for both horse and rider, I had visualized it recorded and passed along for my children and grandchildren (and everyone's grandchildren).

When I returned home and unraveled this tape, I was so pleased to see, captured in print, so much of that day, and that way with the horses.

It was so typical of many other times I had watched Tom work with people and horses. Except for a specific meeting place and time, the horse's needs dictated the schedule of events for this meeting. There was no pressure on either horse or rider to perform a specific maneuver or routine in a certain time. Time became a crystal capsule, every second of it complete. With so much less emphasis on doing, participants were freer *to be*, and to be aware of all the horse had to offer. In an atmosphere where the horse can not "do wrong," there is little pressure for the rider to "do right." With the mind unlocked from a *right* and *wrong* vise, there is more opportunity to be aware.

As you approach the appendix, lean against the corral fence, *be there* on a clear spring day with no role to play except to be aware.

1. *Be aware* of "how the life is coming through the horse's body."

2. *Be aware* of the importance of "riding the horse, straight out, right between your hands and legs." *The life comes through straight.*

3. Be aware of where the horse needs "a little support, a little directing, a little help."

4. *Be aware* of the good—and "leave the good the horse is doing and help him build the weak."

5. Be aware that "if the horse doesn't feel like he is quite all together, *that's OK*, as long as the rider keeps track of what's happening." *It may take quite a while for the horse to get just right on.*

6. Be aware and be "more ready to help the horse at the time the horse needs the help."

7. Be aware of "when the horse is going to *make it anyway*, how important it is for the rider *not to get in the horse's way*."

8. Be aware and "watch for the most opportune time, when it is most fitting for the horse to learn."

9. Be aware that "before you ever start to reach to ask the horse to do something you should have in mind what you are asking and where you are trying to direct and support."

10. Be aware that "you are trying to work with the naturalness the horse was born with. You are just trying to put it to use for you."

—Milly Hunt Porter

Preparing Is the Important Part

Learning how to prepare is very important for both the person and the horse to understand. Horses get a set pattern right early, either right or left, because if you go to catch them it is on the left. If you go to leave, you go that way. You get on on the left and off on the left. These are all things that help establish a fixed pattern pretty quickly with most horses. It is just like a right or left handed person. Pretty soon you are right or left handed, and it is the same with horses. So, the thing to watch for, if they get tipped one way a little too strong, is see if you can help them so they are tipped a little stronger the other way.

When Butler brought his other filly over here a month or so ago, she was strong on the left. She was a little more bothered than this filly. He came by with her yesterday. He had been thinking of that. He had been working on it, and she was strong on the right. But that is OK. See, he will get her evened out. When he asks her to change from one to the other, her whole body and mind will be in that direction, whichever he is asking for.

This filly is a little strong on the left, and we will watch for that. As she was trotting around there in the circle to the left you could feel her body was fitting the contour of the circle. Now you are going to change directions and go to the right. Now compare the way her body, feet and legs—the whole horse—feels. Watch her head and neck—where it is trying to go.

If everything is trying to get shaped up for the left, then you will try to help her prepare to position for the right side. She was coming pretty good there, but you could still feel she had a little drag. She was using her left eye. Now right there she tipped a little to the right with her eye and head. The mare has been close to that a few times before but that was the first time she let go, and got to thinking about the right eye. Pretty soon it wouldn't matter to her what side.

Sometimes a person doesn't think about these things until it becomes a real problem; then it is harder to overcome. It is easy to get them balanced to start with, when they are as green as she is.

Before you ever get on, you can help the horse learn to prepare for these things. When they are loose, when you are getting them to trot or lope around, at first they will kind of go into the corners. You don't want to over-pressure them, but just enough pressure so that they do not hang up in the corners. They will come on out and around. After a few trips around, they round those corners out, and that helps them for what we are working on here, while the filly is being ridden.

When this filly was first loose here and she was coming around, she asked to change directions. That was the time to let her change. Then they will get so they will round these corners either direction. They position their body on the contour they are following.

They may get to where they are kind of exploring things, and get to where they are taking it pretty good—that is the time to change directions. You watch for it—when the horse starts to thinking about asking for a change in directions. When they are green like that you let them change and then go with it that way.

The thing you have to watch is that they don't go cutting off any old time on you. If they do go trying to work you, carry them on a little, then you *fix it up*. Then they will start to ask, and that is all right. The thing you are trying to help them do is to use their own heads. You are trying to present something and then let them figure out, kind of, how to get there. You are trying to present it in a way it will be easier for them to understand. You are trying to present it at a time, and in a way it will be easier for them to learn.

The thing you are trying to establish is to start to understand the meaning of what you are trying to get them to do. It will have no meaning to the horse to start with. Then they begin to get a little meaning of what it is all about, but they still won't see any purpose for it. After a while they will begin to see a purpose. You are trying to help them develop that understanding.

[**Molly:** The purpose in this case would be how to use their body to go around, how to position, and how to prepare to position for the transition.]

Now, Butler, the last two rounds you made there, you could feel something a little different working there than it was—a little easier. You notice she was going but her head and neck were sort of raising a little. She was pretty straight through the body, but her head and neck were raising a little. She was wanting to slow down and stop. When she got over there she put a little more effort into it and did stop. When they are this green you will let them stop and you will stop with them. So that they learn that is OK.

A fellow asked me, "How do you get them to learn to stop without using a corner or something?" This way there wasn't anything in front of her causing her to stop, but her thought was "stop." These are things I watch for them to get to asking. It looks good to me.

You could have let her stop, maybe, that first time this was presented. Then the filly got over to where she is and she said, "Well, let's stop."

She had kind of experimented, but she had not figured, up until about that time, that probably she would be allowed to stop. She put a little more effort into it and she stopped, and you went along with it, which was all right.

Now she's been there three or four minutes in the same tracks, and she isn't scared. She is not there for fear of moving. It feels good to her just to be standing there. She is not afraid of you. You can pet her, move on her, and she will stay there. That is good.

Now that she knows she can stop and isn't afraid to stop, isn't afraid of the rider, you need to handle this situation so that you are in command or she may call the shots. Then she could get cranky if you ask her to go on. She may ask to stop but she won't be shutting it off until you get to the spot where she feels like she would stop—then you will let her know it is all right for the rider to stop there. She may speed up for a while, and then she will sort of test you and ask, "Is it going to be all right to stop or do we go on?" Well, maybe you'll go on a little—then if she is kind of feeling and thinking of waiting for you to ask her to stop—then you will go right along with her. Ask her to stop and let her do as much of the stopping as you can. All you will be trying to do is to keep her straight and even, with as little effort as you can. The less directing you have to do, the better for them. Sometimes you have to do quite a bit of directing; other times it's hardly any. Just try to keep them from turning crooked, or getting crossway, or chopping off, or getting chargey.

Now will you move her out again? We'll see what she is thinking and how she reacts—and take it from there. Now before you start to ask her to move, you are thinking of trying to help her stay straight, so that she doesn't turn her head to the right hand side, or the left hand side.

If you get to checking and watching different horses, so many times you will find when the rider starts to reach to ask them to go forward, that horse will turn its head one way or the other before it starts its feet.

It is liable to always be on the same side if the rider has not noticed it. You watch the head and neck. Now she is standing there straight. When you reach, you try to reach so that the head and neck will stay straight. She was straight.

[**Molly:** Now she is kind of interested in us, but if he were alone, she would likely look off there straight ahead. Now she is looking ahead.]

That would be a good opportunity. You make use of these opportunities when they are green. It helps them when you try to make it as easy for them as you can. You watch for the opportune time, when it is most fitting for them to learn.

Now when you reach just give her time. She still wants to go over. She wants to turn her head to the left. It does not matter whether she moves out of her tracks. We are watching this part. Just let down— start from scratch. Don't try to really move her because we are watching that head and neck. It is so important at this stage of the game, and all through. She wants to cross over, that's all right. You can let her tip to the right a little. If you would try to keep her too straight, too exact—she may get hung up and wouldn't know what to do.

You will let her head tip a little to the right side, she has been so definitely trying to get it to the left. So, when she quits trying to get it to the left, maybe she will tip it to the right. Then you'll try to get her feet to come, so that she will know she can move when she tips away from the left.

She is good for us to work on this. She is not calloused but you can definitely see she has a pattern. On her it won't take very long because she is not disturbed—she wants to be all right. It is just a matter of her learning how to separate this.

She does not have to move her feet yet. You will be able to feel a change all through her body here pretty soon when you reach for her.

When you have been reaching, the whole horse has been prepared to position for the left. Now this last time she was not putting quite as much effort into that, and she was starting to soften. She put her head around to the right. She was almost ready to move a foot. At this time she does not really know what to do. She does not see the meaning in this. She doesn't get the meaning of what this is being asked for. She is quite a ways from seeing a purpose—that will come later. The only reason she is doing anything right, is she doesn't know what else to do. When she started to put her head to the left, she came up against pressure. The person tries to arrange so the pressure the horse comes in contact with is from the horse and allows the horse to learn to yield to the pressure the horse is putting on itself. She put it over to the right to get away from pressure. She still does not have the meaning of getting her feet to go. She has to pick that up next. To get the meaning, when she starts to the left and gets pressure and yields to that, then the rider tries to help direct and encourage her to go forward. Pretty soon she won't have to tip to the left, or to the right. As you reach, those feet will come right on through, straight and centered. That is when she begins to get some meaning of what is being asked. A little later she sees the purpose—get going so they can do something else.

This is something if you want to just practice a little. Just go out to the center; we'll be able to watch better. The filly stopped in a left hand position. Now if she started, she is in position to start in the left hand position. If you ask her to start forward from there, shift to the right hand position, so that she will get going to the right. The way she is now she may be ready to shift, and maybe not. We'll watch and see.

You'll be thinking before you reach—before you even reach to ask her to move forward or to the right—you are thinking about the position she is in now. You can feel that. So, now you are trying to help her prepare to position for the opposite to what she is in—which in a way will be a transition from the left to the right.

I think from where we are working now, from where she is at this point, you will fix it up so she will yield to your right. So you go into the right hand direction. That's fine. Just let it teeter there a little so Molly can watch. Don't hurry it—she'll explore. She is still trying to get in the left hand position. Even though she gave a little to the right, and started to prepare to position for that, she swung back to her left. It just doesn't feel comfortable to her. Try it again. She was still thinking left. That was closer. You only ask. If she gives a step or two the way you want, that is enough at this time.

It is easier to keep track of what is taking place, when you are comparing the two sides—that will help them on the side that they need the help, without taking away any good from the better, stronger side. You try to leave the good and help them build the weak.

Just start over again—just draw. You will go down with your right hand first—now she is tipping to the right. Now, again—then she wanted to tip to the left. Just wait there until she yields to the right. Now again—she is hanging, waiting. When she started to put her head around, she wasn't thinking of maybe walking off in that direction. She was thinking of putting her head around there to be petted or something. But when it started around there, got just a start, you could have encouraged the feet to come. That would have helped her get off center right at that time. It would have been an opportunity. It doesn't really matter at this stage because we have plenty of time—but these opportune times help them get directed.

Now reach with your right again—that's fine. Most people are right handed. There are more right handed people than there are left. This is going to sound like it contradicts itself to start with, but one of the reasons horses tip to the left when a right handed person reaches for the right side is when they reach, the timing is not right. When the horse feels the rider reach with the right hand they take ahold of the bit, the halter, or the hackamore. They take ahold of it and tip to the left, against it. The horse ought to be here but there is a timing factor in there that the rider is missing. The horse gets ahold and tips. If the rider has not recognized what took place, or understands that part, then it gets to be a set pattern. When the rider starts to reach, the horse tips against it, instead of yielding, you see.

Now, right from there she is down the middle. Her body, her backbone is straight and she is relaxed. When you reach you will go down the right rein before she has a chance, has time or a chance to tip to the left. That was an opportunity to go down the rein. Wait for her to yield to you. That's fine—you can release the pressure. You notice after she started she was a little unsure, but she did start to yield. After she got a little ways, then she stopped coming on. She kind of tested, raised her head and neck a little—then she let go and came on.

That was good—just fine.

Had you missed the timing when you went to reach—while you were going down—reaching down the rein—she would have already been over to the left by the time you got there. This timing factor is so important.

Now as the horse gets a little more caught up on this feel and timing, the rider gets a little more caught up also. Even if the filly starts to go over to the left, the rider can reach early enough and have time to help the horse start to learn how to position. The approach you take, the feel and timing, the firmness and softness, all blend in there. If she starts over she will come up against that, and she will start to yield to watch that she does not even get started across. The person needs to learn to try to get there early enough—*before it happens.*

I have had people say, "Well how do you get there?" They think they don't have time. Well, they don't, to start with; by the time they act it is too late. The horse has already felt of them before they reach. But that is what they are preparing for, so it's over there and the horse is ahead of them.

I tell them to do just like we are doing here. When the horse is really not aware the person is going to reach, *then*; they go down that rein and they are there before the horse has seen it. Then the horse is liable to yield. Then when you reach he will yield before the pressure ever touches. That is what we are trying to develop.

OK, now's the time to reach.

It was late—by the time I spoke, before I finished, it was too late—then by the time it got to you, and you started to act, it was quite a little late.

[**Molly:** That is what is hard about a situation like this.]

Yes, this is the hard thing here. This is what one is faced with and struggles with to try to get it in print, so these things will be out there loud and clear. So, if a person reads it, they won't miss it. That's what I've been trying to get for fifty years.

Now, she will yield to that—all you had to do was fix and wait. These little things like this are so important to a horse. There is getting to be a little meaning there for her; a while ago there was no meaning. A little meaning is starting to develop.

[**Molly**: When he moves a little she comes that way.]

This is one example of what I mean when I say "meaning." There is starting to be a little meaning for the horse. At this time she sees no purpose for it, but pretty soon when she gets where there is some meaning—then you ask for the feet to go on—to some place where you are directing—then she will see the purpose of this. The purpose is to get where you are directing—to understand the meaning so that you can see the purpose to where you are directing. Now that's sort of a tangled up expression. But, it's untangling these things—trying to help the horse untangle the person. The better the person understands where the horse is and what is going on through the horse's mind and body, the better chance they have of helping the horse untangle things they don't understand. But, a person can be tangled up.

She is a nice filly.

There, you see, she came up against that. She kind of bumped it a little, a couple of times—she came against her own pressure. You had it fixed so that if she didn't yield, she went against the pressure she applied to herself. Then when she discovered she was putting that pressure on herself, she moved away from it and her feet came. *Just that!* You saw that right there.

This is the whole story, right there. You are trying to present it so if they don't yield, they put the pressure on themselves. And you are trying to allow them the opportunity to get it separated to realize they are putting the pressure on themselves, so they will yield to that pressure.

She was tangled some earlier, but what is taking place here now is doing both the horse and the rider more good than going out here riding for five miles, at this stage of the game. Now you can reach with your right hand, go down the rein, and her head will come on around.

[**Molly:** Even though her attention was over to the left.]

Yes. As Butler was starting down there she was yielding.

[**Molly:** She has already learned to look for it.]

Now again—see, there's no "rocks" in the way—no hard spots. She came around smooth, and she will get even smoother. The thing you are trying to do is for the message to go right to the feet. Pretty soon now you will see this.

When the rider reaches, the feet are getting ready. It's just like you try to bypass everything else and go direct from your thoughts to their feet—and those feet yield.

When you have control of the feet and legs without resistance, the body is supple, but if there is stiffness in the horse anywhere, there is stiffness every place.

Now don't have the tendency to want to hurry and not let her find it. You fix and wait for them to find it. It is their idea when they move that foot.

[**Molly:** Now he's just pretty much sitting quiet with this.]

This is the thing that you are feeling. There, see how those feet are starting? The message is starting to register in the feet. When you reach you already know where you are asking them to go. Before you ever start to reach to ask them to do something—you should have in mind *what that is*, and where you are trying to direct—direct and support.

[**Molly:** Where you want that foot to travel. But you are not doing anything physical at this point; you're just thinking about it, right?]

Well, in order to answer that question—a person has no idea how much feel that horse has. How little that goes on in the person's mind and body that horse is feeling—that the person is not even close to being aware of. So, in trying to answer your question about the body feel—they are feeling that—and if that body is just sitting there dull and dead without any meaning—why, they feel that. But you don't have to be doing a lot of physical action for the horse to get the message, if that's what you are asking—where you are trying to direct them and support.

There are times that it takes everything you have, both physical and mental, to help them get over these rough spots. The other extreme is, it is so little, you are doing so little. It is such a delicate feel and timing, that it is hardly measurable. That is where we are trying to work.

This is what I try to get people to recognize and realize. Most people get a lot of activity and all that, you see, a lot of physical activity. They are strong on that, and a horse is liable to get that way too. But this part here, that most people bypass, is the part that I am trying to bring out loud and clear. It is so important. But if there isn't some life and meaning, and feel and timing, this isn't any good either. You don't have anything but a blank.

It doesn't matter whether it is slow sitting there—slow walk—a faster walk—a slow trot—a faster trot—slow lope—a fast lope, or a dead run. This thing that we are talking about, trying to bring out here, is the same, regardless of what the speed is—or if you get to the peak of the run and then you start back down. It is just the same, this feel. Some people get along good when they are out going real fast; other people get along better just poking along. But this will operate all the way if a person understands how to help a horse understand it.

[**Molly:** But you want to start here?]

This is the place I like to start. Now there are horses that have a build up and have a lot of go; then it is better to let them go than try to confine them too close. They can't stand it, there is an explosive spot. So it is better to go and work from there back to where you can start on this area we have been working. It doesn't really matter. What fits one horse might not fit the other. The approach you take—you are trying to adjust to the situation that best fits the occasion.

Now, you can ask her to back up a little. Looks like she is wanting to do something, even if it is to eat a bite of grass. The same thing again, you just let her find it. You just notice her head and neck raises and her nose goes out a little and up.

If you want to, just wait right there. Just take the pressure off and let her start again. In order to back up, those feet have to yield. Wait right there; she would rather not back up. She was backing up some but she would rather not. Instead of the message getting to those feet, and they get free, she was trying to escape through the head. Now if you like, go forward so she is not in that low spot, or so close to the fence, so she has more room. When they are that green, if the fence is fifteen feet it looks like it is too close. That looks better. She has a two way deal there for an escape behind. She could go to the right or left and have room to go. That other way she was liable to start to the right or left before she got going.

Now reach to ask her to back, and think about keeping her head and neck pretty much centered, and her body pretty well straight—as best you can. You won't have to over-insist, and you'll wait for those feet, that is far enough. You can see that she started to get over to the right behind, and before she would be free for the step to back up she would come up against her own pressure.

Now we will run that again. We will wait for the feet. That looked better—that's far enough. It was three steps in a row, and she is ready for the fourth one, in position for the fourth one, and she stayed pretty straight.

She was trying to explore for an escape, relief—but she wasn't pushing. She was yielding through the feet and legs, and her body was not getting crooked. Now if it does that well, it can't help but get better.

OK now, you want to make another start. She is starting to prepare. Now, she is starting to get over to the right behind a little. Go forward—straight forward. Don't try to ask her to stop now because she is wanting to be crooked. Until her feet kind of get over behind, don't ask them to stop. If you have room, keep drifting until her body straightens; *then* try to help her stop. When she is getting over there and getting crooked, she is not understanding how to straighten up and stop. All that does is just put more crook in.

Now reach again. It feels like now if she tried to do anything she would try to move toward the right behind. So, you are thinking of that before you ever start.

[A pickup and trailer rattle by on the road close to the corral.]

Now—wait a little bit there—that excitement—Now WATCH! WATCH! When she wanted to turn over this way, Butler, if you would have kept her here you would have gotten a good reach behind. See—you could have used that, because she wanted to see what that was. If you could have kept her on this side of the line, she would have given a step or two. Then you could have let her look. She would have learned there, without even thinking what she was doing, to yield those feet and legs—and that's important. If you would have held that feel there she would have had to move in order to look because she just had to look. It was all ready to come.

I am not saying you didn't do right. I am only trying to bring out, there was an opportunity to help her learn something.

[**Tom Butler:** Yes, I could feel it too.]

You could feel it and had we experienced this before that came along, you would have done it. It just looked like you wanted to do it, and I thought for a bit you were going to put that to work for you—but you didn't understand there was meaning there.

[**Molly:** That is part of the complication of this kind of a situation.]

When that commotion came I started to say, "That's good, we can put that to work for us," but it does give us a talking point. These are things that are so important to watch for—the opportune time to just let things happen. The horse doesn't know how he learned it. It is there and it is well established. These things get very effective. You are trying to work with the naturalness the horse is born with. You are just trying to help them put it to use.

Just now, Butler, right there she came around, and she was bent, and her last step was off to the left—she kind of wobbled—see, she is teetery.

Have you raised chickens? You have seen those young roosters when they get up about so big—then they try to learn how to crow. Sometimes they hop up on something and they will be a little wobbly getting up there. Then they get to thinking they are going to crow—they pretty near tip off—and wobble again. Finally they get to where they can flop their wings up there, but when they start to crow they wobble again. But pretty soon they hop up there, flap their wings and crow—without a wobble. That is the same thing this filly is going through. The young rooster stage—it is the wobbly stage. You put up with that; you understand what it is; and then that's all there is to it. As time goes on you try to help them position so they can keep their balance for the next step, or the one they have just finished. So they will be balanced, so they can be in a position to take a step or not to take it or change directions—or whatever.

The balance part is so important. That word *balance*; it can be thought of, interpreted, quite a lot of ways. What I'm thinking of is like this: that's really what it all turns out to *is* balance.

Now she looks good. She looks great, wouldn't you say, Molly?

[**Molly:** I was going to mention, you know that sleepy look about the time her feet started to move when he would take her head to the right; that look has left her eye.]

That's right—they will go through that spot. Before they start to get some meaning to what it is all about, they let down. In a way they are a little bewildered. They don't know much what to do. Pretty soon those feet will start to come alive and then they have something to look forward to.

[**Molly:** Reminds me of being in some class at school. When I didn't understand the class I would get sleepy; but if I understood I would be OK.]

Very same thing as what you saw in this filly. Exactly the same thing. So the person that is trying to help the horse tries to help them come out of that.

[**Molly:** That is a place I have really missed. I have seen that look on so many colts and I have thought they weren't paying attention. You know?]

You didn't know what to do.

[**Molly:** I'd get after them and they were just glassy-eyed with not knowing what was going on.]

That's exactly right.

A couple fellows from Montana were here the last of January. They came on Wednesday evening. The neighbor fellow came over the same evening. We visited a while. What the neighbor wanted to know was if we could come over when he started some colts. There were five of them. The next morning the three of us went over about eight. We left about five. We didn't stop for lunch.

[**Molly:** That's a day's worth.]

There were just five colts. They were pretty good to work with. But we took quite a bit of time. I didn't expect it to be any other way because we took time to try to help bring out these little spots.

The fellow wrote a couple of weeks ago. He was in South Dakota at a friend's place. They had about twenty colts they had been working with. He said he got a lot out of his trip. He said he had spent a lot of time just sitting on those colts, kind of understanding them a little bit. He said the horses seemed to like him a lot better than they had ever liked him before. Now, that has its place for a while. You see! When he learns, kind of, what is taking place then he can create the activity with control and meaning and progress. Some of these things here are just what he needed. But there comes a time when you need to put in a little more life and activity in there, so that it will carry on and build.

Margaret is coming [on horseback]—there, the filly is looking—she is not scared—she is alert. These are opportune times; you can back, go forward or whatever you want to do. It is like when the rig went by a while ago. You make use of these opportune times.

You can reach with your right hand now; she is centered. Now: she is coming on. It was just an instant, but there really was no hang up—that was good. Now she will yield again, and see, her feet are coming. Pretty soon when you reach, the life will be in those feet—that pause won't be there. You can stop, withdraw, any time, without moving the feet; or you can increase that and the feet will come alive faster. This is where you get the control, when the message gets to the feet. When you get the control of the feet, the rest is easy.

Now just a minute. Margaret, do you want to just start on around [the outside of the corral]? Butler will just go right on around; that's what I wanted to see. See how the filly hooked on. You watch for these things—it can be a dog, or a calf, or a cow, or another horse, or a rock or anything.

[**Molly:** Do you mean early on?]

Yes, or any time.

[**Molly:** Oh really!]

You never want to forget that.

[**Molly:** But how about when the horse kind of wants to go with the other horses, and that really isn't what you want to do?]

The horse will be with you. This brings that all through, you see. It was so easy for the horse to move its feet—its body. There were no stiff spots anyplace. It was just all together. If the rider didn't want to go there, he would let this thing that you saw develop there, up to where everything was there. Then if he didn't want to go with the filly the rider could keep that with him and just come on around. It is a little easier said than done. But when you really understand it, it is just as easy to do as to say.

[**Molly:** Well, I am starting to know what you mean; but making it my own—I haven't got that part.]

Well, you still have to learn how, just as the horse has to learn. If you start to do something with your left hand that you haven't been used to doing, even though you know what you want to do, you still have to get your reflexes so they will respond to what you are thinking.

I can throw a rope at a calf, I think I can, about as good as ever, thinking about what I want to do; but I can't get it done. Because things just don't work like they did at one time. Once in a while I get things timed just right, and if the movement fits my speed it looks about as good as it ever did. But if it doesn't, I can't catch up. I can't make the transition in the time it needs to make it, even though I am thinking of it and trying it—it just doesn't work, and that is something I'm not going to get any better at. Old age has set in.

[**Molly:** That's kind of discouraging.]

Yes!

Now, while you are talking with Butler, Margaret, just move to your left. This is a good exercise for that right side.

Just let her go, Butler, see how she's hooked on; that helps get the right eye. She is learning to use that, and she doesn't even know she is learning. But it is working. When you can get these things to work, that is more valuable than having to make a project out of it. As they get further along, you put them into situations where it is necessary for them to find their way out. They have some basics then to go on. They have learned to yield to the person.

When the horse is green you go kind of where it is easiest for the horse—you go with him. Then as time goes on you get the horse to accompany you. The next step is you are accompanying each other.

At the twenty-five [ranch] in Nevada when I would help start those colts, they would have from thirty up to forty each fall. We would put in about a month.

John and Freddie would each get on a green colt. We had about five loose horses in the corral, too. That was enough; it seemed to fit pretty good because they were green too. I would be on horseback. I'd tell those boys, just kind of go with the loose horses. The colts they were on were wanting to go with the loose horses. When the colts with a rider on them headed for the other horses they wanted to get out of there— so they would move. The loose ones were trying to get away, and the others were trying to catch up. There would be quite a little activity.

[**Molly:** Yeah, I'll bet!]

All I tried to do was to keep everything going in the same direction so there wouldn't be a clash—a crash. Then, when it came time for a change in direction I'd try to bend these horses at the time they wouldn't run into each other. After a little of that, going different directions, those colts the boys were on would find out it wasn't so important to get with the other horses. The boys would watch, and when the colts would want to cut off, or change directions or do something else, I told those boys not to try to go anywhere except where the horse went, to start with—go right with them. Just like they were riding them there. Just like that was what they wanted them to do; maybe help them just a little.

[**Molly:** You'd be trying to figure out what the horse was going to do, but probably you'd be just a tad behind the horse.]

Well, those boys, to start with, were two or three tads behind. You let the horse sort of make the decision. It would be the horse's idea, you see, and you would go right along with it. It was just like you were guiding it there, but you were not putting the pressure on or forcing the issue. It was like that was exactly what you wanted to do. You tried to tie that in as close to the timing with the horse's thoughts as the rider could adjust to.

[**Molly:** So the rider was making all the effort to get with the horse?]

That's right. Go with the horse. You are accompanying the horse. Then pretty soon the horse begins to find out it isn't so important, such a necessity, to get with the other horses for security and cover. He isn't relying on that so strong.

A little later when those horses were coming around I'd bend those loose ones, and the boys could take their horse right on by and out around.

[**Molly:** Was that still the horse's idea?]

You had to support and direct, but you were getting the horse to learn to accompany you.

[**Molly:** Already! Even in that time?]

It didn't take very many trips around before we were kind of ready for this. While they were still coming with the horses, the boys were still getting the horse to know where they were. The horse was learning to find the rider and to respond to the rider some. When the time was right you set this up, and the horses were not hooked so strong with the loose horses. Then if the rider started early enough to let the horse know they were going to ride on by, they would just ride right out there like it was nothing. That, I think, is what you were asking a while ago. First you come with the horse; when you are doing that you are developing communication. Then when you get to where the horse will communicate with you, from then on you get it so you communicate with each other. But you are in command. You might yield some for a while until the horse got it figured out—what you wanted to do—so you were getting together. But you are trying to accompany each other. That is the third thing. This isn't easy for people to picture, all of it, how important these things are for the horse.

Now, Butler, you can reach for the other side while she is still moving. See those little uptight spots? Pretty soon those will smooth right out and you will be able to go either direction. You can work a little on that if you want to, Butler. Just start out—that direction first, just from where you are.

Now let her straighten out and go straight forward for a while. She wants to cross over to the left. See how the feet are uncertain? Sort of meaningless steps—she doesn't know just what to do about it. Not very many of those steps feel secure.

[**Tom Butler:** No, they are jerky.]

Take her around. Pretty soon you will feel a change.

[**Tom Butler:** She is trying to fold up there in the middle, kind of.]
Use the other direction for a while—that is getting better.

Before, I mentioned to you to set right down with the horse; you were riding on past when she was going to stop anyway. You were not giving her an opportunity to feel you prepare to stop—you were riding on past. She was thinking of going on, and you were thinking of stopping.

Go again—you are not going to ask her to stop now—right there keep working your feet and legs and keep just behind that center line—feet and legs—ride her right out between your hands and legs. This may take just a little while. There she is over that little hump. You rolled her up over it and then she went. That is the other side of stopping. You let them know to stop, or you let them know to go on. But don't get ahead of those feet. There is a line right there. I usually say you will feel it right behind the saddle horn, right straight across in front of you. If you are wanting them to go on, don't get over that line; stay behind that line. You will work your feet until the feet go—stay just behind the driving point and drive.

Now start her off—that's it—use your right rein just a little. Looks good, right there. Keep coming forward—now draw and release—there, that's it. If you don't release they get to leaning on it. If they tetter on it, you let them come up against that pressure. That's good—that's it—that's good enough.

Now ride her on again—now ride her on—ride her on—ride her on. Now ease off and let her stop. See how she stuck her right hind leg under.

Where I said, "Ride her on," then by the time she got over there she was going all smooth and I said, "Let her stop." Everything just fell into place. This is what takes care of that spot you were asking about. How you can keep them from stopping when you don't want to. They learn to yield. They are accompanying the rider, then you accompany each other. It's all that simple. So simple it's difficult.

That was a good test. This is the way to get them to go right on by and leave other horses just like they weren't there. The main thing is to start early to let them know you are asking them to go right on by.

[**Molly:** In a case where you weren't here, how would the rider create the original life?]

The rider could maybe work this where the situation will not require as much coming from him to start with. It wouldn't be very long until Butler wouldn't need me there—even from where she was to start with.

Right now I was filling in a little so if he missed a little or was a little late, I would fill in so she would carry until he could get it himself. That was all I was doing. But as he got caught up he wouldn't need me at all—he could bury me.

The first important thing is to think about riding them straight out—right between your hands and your legs from where she is now. See—the life came through her straight. That is what takes care of what I was doing out there—I was filling in. Pretty soon she will respond to the rider—she wouldn't need me.

[**Molly:** Boy! You really have to concentrate!]

It's pretty hard to keep track of the feel and the timing and what the horse's thoughts are. When the rider gets a better understanding of communication you don't have to think so much about it; it gets kind of like breathing. Like this filly today near the last; when they came around, you could kind of see she wanted to tip to the left, but he kept her going. Butler was doing enough to keep her coming on. If he hadn't, she would have turned, you see. After you get the feel of these things—before the horse gets too far, you can feel it *almost* going to happen—before it starts—then you start to do something. You don't have to think what you are going to do. Those are the things I think you kind of have to develop. For different individuals it seems to work a little different.

In working with somebody, or trying to help them with something, I find it isn't easy for me to get them to work in the area where it seems like they need to work. *They keep trying to work at the end result.*

A while back, I was working with a girl on the change of leads. She is doing pretty well now. Well, five or six years ago she had that in mind—the flying change. But I kept trying to get her to work away back there where the horse could be in position for the change, where he would be prepared to position for the transition. But that meant nothing much to her. A change of leads was what she was looking for. So, that is what she was applying her efforts on—a change of leads. She wasn't preparing to position for it—just change leads.

I was trying to get her to work on this, and not try to get the change of leads unless it just happened to shape up so it was all right. But that did not mean much to her on that. She was trying to change the lead. When *she* got ready to change the lead regardless of where the *horse* was, she wanted to change leads.

It took quite a while before she realized the preparing was the important part, even though I would say it over and over. Once she got the picture, it was easy. When she understood when the horse was in position for the change, she just let it happen. Then she really got the feel, timing, and balance.